Theatre in the Ca

Ken Corsbie

Introduction by Trevor Rhone

Tony Boxill

Thanks for meet g you
Good luck in all
[signature]
'92

HODDER AND STOUGHTON

LONDON SYDNEY AUCKLAND TORONTO

Contents

Preface   iii

Introduction   iv

Chapter 1   Theatre everywhere   1
Chapter 2   Speechifying and storytelling   3
Chapter 3   Poetry as drama   8
Chapter 4   Plays for everybody   16
Chapter 5   Plays, players and playwrights 25
Chapter 6   Dance as theatre   32
Chapter 7   Musical theatre   36
Chapter 8   Other forms   43
Chapter 9   Sharing   48
Chapter 10   Theatre tomorrow   52

Glossary   55

For
Daphne
Len
Kim
and Nigel

Corsbie, Ken
    Theatre in the Caribbean.
    1. Theatre—Caribbean Area—History
    I. Title
    792'.09182'1   PN2390

ISBN 0 340 32954 8

First published 1984
Copyright © 1984 by Ken Corsbie

Photoset by Rowland Phototypesetting Ltd
Bury St Edmunds, Suffolk

Printed in Great Britain for Hodder and Stoughton Educational, a division of Hodder and Stoughton Ltd, Mill Road, Dunton Green, Sevenoaks, Kent by St Edmundsbury Press, Bury St Edmunds, Suffolk.

Acknowledgments

The author and publishers are grateful to the following for permission to reproduce photographs in this book:

Christopher Pearce (Panic Pictures) (page vi); Willie Alleyne (pages 4, 12 and 31); Black Theatre Canada, Toronto (page 9); Caribbean Broadcasting Corporation of Barbados (page 45); Ken Corsbie (pages 9, 21, 23, 26, 28, 41, 46, 50 and 51); Tye King (page 6); Mark Lyndersay (pages 22 and 42); Ruth Moore (page 40); Keith Morrison (page 30); People's Action Theatre, Dominica (pages 38 and 39); Reds Perreira (page 53); Pat Pierre (pages 11 and 20); Kingsley Roberts (page 13); Ed Rodway (pages iii, 2, 17, 19 and 24); Ken Sue-Wing (pages 14 and 44); Robert Wakefield (page 34); Eugene Williams (page 49); Ann Goerdt for the photograph of Ken Corsbie on the back cover; John Agard and Paul Keens-Douglas for the extracts from their poems.

The author and publishers would also like to acknowledge the use of the following photographs on the cover: top left: *Ti-Jean and his Brothers* by Derek Walcott. A Stage-One Production, Barbados, produced by Michael Gilkes; top right: *Midnight Robber'* designed by Peter Minshall in Trinidad; bottom right: *Brashana O* by Gloria Lannarman. Produced by the Little Theatre Movement of Jamaica; bottom left: *King Jab-Jab* from an All Theatre Production directed by Helen Camps.

Finally, the author would like to acknowledge the assistance of the following: all the theatre practitioners and friends in the Caribbean with whom he has collaborated over the last ten years; Diane Chun of the Gainesville *Sun* newspaper in Florida who helped with the dotting of the i's and the crossing of the t's, and all those who responded to his requests for information and photographs.

Every effort has been made to trace and acknowledge ownership of copyright. The publishers will be glad to make suitable arrangements with any copyright holders whom it has not been possible to contact.

From *Journey to Freedom* written by Francis Farrier, Guyana, 1976.

Preface

Theatre in the Caribbean will concern itself with the English speaking Caribbean – from Belize on the Central American coast, through the island chain down to Guyana on the coast of South America. It will include the Bahamas, Cayman Islands, US and British Virgin Islands, Jamaica, Leewards and Windwards, Barbados, Trinidad and Tobago. As an exception, we will include some aspects of theatre in Surinam, the former Dutch colony.

In the book **Music in the Caribbean*** which was the first in this series, you learned how music played a most important part in people's lives. *Theatre in the Caribbean* makes the same point.

There are three kinds of theatre which will be discussed:
- the first and most important is made up by the exciting and interesting things people do in their everyday lives.
- the second covers the festivals and rituals with which we celebrate our history and our religions.
- finally there are the planned performances done especially for audiences to enjoy.

Carnival is theatre, and a wedding is theatre. A cricket match, car accident, fire, argument, discotheque, court scene, laughter in the school yard, your classroom – all are the theatre of everyday life. Theatre can also be a jazz concert, political meeting, street preacher, end-of-term school play, a football match, a stick-fight, and the dance and song recitals in the local Community centre.

Like our music, our theatre is unique because we have unique origins or roots, and we have mixed these roots in very special ways. Those origins come from Africa, Europe, Asia, America, and also from the first people in these islands, the Amerindians.

We hope you will see how the formal theatre, with its stage and auditorium and lights, is usually a direct result of how we think and live day by day. We will also show you where some of the techniques and styles which we use on the formal stages come from. Finally you will know more about what kinds of dramatic plays are being performed today in the Caribbean.

We can only briefly point to some of the many dramatic factors which make up our ways of living, and the way they influence our more formal theatre performances. If you become interested in finding out more, perhaps you will carry out your own research into the theatre in the Caribbean.

*Please see page **55**.

Introduction

I thought I'd read another book in the series, *Music in the Caribbean*, before writing this introduction. After a long search I found the text on my seven-year old's bookshelf. She wanted to know what I wanted with her book. I explained about *Theatre in the Caribbean*. She was delighted and eagerly awaits the publication. For her it will be another book to be read, enjoyed, then added to her growing Caribbean collection.

I was struck by this contrast with my early years, when the word 'Theatre' was never part of one's vocabulary; and when it became so many years later, it meant the place where movies were shown. Yet, one was never short of entertainment: story telling, speechifying, extemporizing and riddles were just some of the early traditions that *Theatre in the Caribbean* records. The 'Tea Party' that Ken Corsbie mentions, I knew in Jamaica as 'Pleasant Sunday Afternoon', which in time grew into the 'Tea Meeting', a more secular event. I especially enjoyed the 'Tea Meeting', where members of the community gathered at the shop 'paeza' (piazza) and sang, recited or played on their home-made musical instruments. Performances were heckled or cheered by the audience – 'Sixpence to take that singer down . . .!'; 'Ninepence to put him back up . . .!' – and much fun was had by all.

I suspect that there was where my love for the 'Theatre' was born, but at that time, I simply wanted to become an entertainer; and to become an entertainer, one had to move away from one's traditions, go to the U.K., Europe or the U.S., and learn from alien models.

So, at the end of three very impressionable years at an English Drama School, having received the best possible training in theatre, and having absorbed it fully, I was back home – 'to show them'! My first production was a double bill – Strindberg's *Miss Julie* and Edward Albee's *The Zoo Story*. In a possible house of five hundred, we had an audience of *four*! It was devastating. Where had I gone wrong? I had successfully submerged my way of speaking, thinking, doing, and had become the accomplished mimic – I spoke the Queen's English perfectly; I was an authority on Chaucer – 'This gentil' cock had in his governaunce seven hens to doon all his plesaunce . . .'. I saw myself as a great Shakespearean tragedian actor in the Henry Irvine mould. I had done everything to succeed. How well I had forgotten the words of the great Trinidadian actor Edric Connor, 'Whatever they teach you in England, forget half of it!'

Here I was on the horn of a dilemma, and there were no Caribbean models, no heroes, to help me chart a new course.

My next effort was the product of a blind, irrational decision to break all the rules. This took one back to the time when 'much fun was had by all', and, to my surprise, it was a huge success. Comments from the audience were most revealing; 'Boy, I could really relate to that', 'Man that was my life story', 'It cleared up a lot of things in my head'. Yet for me, the production was not totally satisfying. I had discarded all the valid things I had learnt in the U.K. It was then that Edric Connor's advice became clear to me, and I began a process of selection, for there was much I could learn from the alien models and usefully apply to my own situation. From that point I was able to move forward successfully.

If at the age of seven, I had had a book like *Theatre in the Caribbean* as a point of reference, I would have avoided that tortuous journey away from self. Hopefully this book will help others to avoid similar pitfalls.

Corsbie's book records the progress of theatre in the Caribbean. Acts of faith and a great deal of courage by many in the region have set our theatre on a very positive course. In many of our islands it is an industry, or fast becoming so. As Corsbie documents, it is the only source of income for a number of our peoples.

But most importantly, our theatre is helping to restore the spirit of the Caribbean man – as it helps to topple old negative images and set in place more meaningful ones; to identify and establish past models and heroes who can be a source of inspiration and strength in our present daily struggles. Caribbean theatre has become today a source of pride. It is one area of our lives in which we are genuinely beginning to applaud each other. Standing ovations are no longer reserved for the players from outside.

But there are threats to ongoing development. One has to be aware that the pitfalls, which existed when I was seven, still exist today, and in an even more menacing form. While I chose to leave my environment to absorb a foreign culture, today this is being beamed to us; twenty-four hours a day we are being bombarded with alien values and alien models. In the Caribbean one can spend an entire evening watching television, and be fed an almost total diet of fare that bears no relevance at all to our situation. Saddest of all is to see a local anchorman lost for words as he gropes for superlatives to encourage you to watch some second-rate meaningless film that glorifies some mythical foreign folk hero.

One agrees with Ken Corsbie, that 'Television drama costs more to produce locally than to rent from abroad – and also needs special skills and expensive technical equipment.' At the same time, we need to enter the market place, not just as buyers, but as sellers. There is a global demand for good television programmes, and returns could be tenfold. I believe that our television stations need to rethink their positions, take an imaginative leap and start producing now for the immediate markets that exist within the Caribbean islands. This interchange would help much to bridge the isolation gaps that exist between our territories at this time.

The search for a Caribbean form should be one of our priorities at this time, but soaring production costs and lack of adequate theatre space are really beginning to slow development, and there is little experimentation taking place. To quote a young playwright: 'Boy this new play better do well, if not the Bank coming for me.' So at this time, many producers are taking the path of minimum risk and staging tried and often trite material. There is much talk of recession, inflation, devaluation, but we cannot afford to devalue ourselves nor the creative urges that may be our one source of salvation in these harsh economic times.

As we search for areas in our lives to foster growth and expand development, I join with Ken Corsbie: 'If all the schools had a full programme of Theatre Arts as a part of their everyday curricula, then perhaps, the Caribbean would have theatre for everybody.' Many of our schools are aware, and have full time specialist teachers, but one of the problems with teaching theatre has been the absence of a relevant text. Students measure the importance of a subject by the number of texts the subject requires; they are accustomed to a certain discipline, and having a text is part of that discipline. *Theatre in the Caribbean* will help to solve that problem. And if we start with the primary schools, theatre can become a powerful tool for growth and edification, and will help to mould and change, to direct and forge new paths for the Caribbean peoples.

And as one looks ahead to tomorrow and the unknown, one is thankful for *Theatre in the Caribbean*. My one regret is that there was not such a book before, that documented more of the past. As Corsbie says, 'The future is built upon the past . . .' We have lost whole areas of our lives that we could have drawn on to help chart our future.

But one should not dwell on this loss; let us join together as a Caribbean people, support each other, draw from each other's strengths and learn from our weaknessess, so that we can be better able to face the future and deal with it.

Perhaps one can draw from one of the most moving theatrical experiences of our everyday life – the *Nine Night* ceremony, performed at a time when one is faced with another sort of loss:

> One can still hear the sound of song *The Sankey*, as one approaches; the notes are full of hope, cheer and comfort; the voices are not hushed but triumphant – Call and Response, Call and Response. The singing echoes through the valleys and is carried by the wind; and fear and uncertainty are replaced by confidence and courage . . .

And if one listens to the wind today, one can hear the voices – Edric Connor, Derek Walcott, Beryl McBurnie, Louise Bennett, Noel Vaz, Rex Nettleford, and others – who must have travelled their own tortuous journeys, but through faith and courage are helping to give us all a sense of hope. And above the hum, one can hear the voice of Ken Corsbie who has taken the time, the care and the trouble to record the voices that will help to lead us away from the negative toward a more creative path – the total realization of self – and 'much fun will be had by all'.

Trevor D. Rhone
September 1983

A scene in *Smile Orange*, probably Trevor Rhone's most famous play. This picture is taken from a performance of the play at the Tricycle Theatre in London in 1983. This illustrates the growing international market for Caribbean theatre.

1 Theatre is everywhere

A one-time fast bowler is telling an old cricket story to a young man. He shows his run-up and describes a special tour during which he was bypassed for selection into the West Indies test team. His dramatic flair, language, movements and theme have the one-man audience spellbound. In the neighbouring yard can be heard someone whistling the 1950 calypso **Cricket Lovely Cricket**. That situation is everyday theatre in the Caribbean.

A policeman comes into a tenement yard to arrest the poor father of a young girl for stealing $70.00. There is a very sad moment when mother, father and frightened daughter hold each other as the lawman announces the charge. It is an agonizing drama which is unfortunately played out in real life too often in the Caribbean.

A young tramcar driver decides to leave home and go to England in search of a better life. He has no intentions of coming back to the ghetto yard. He is telling his girl friend for the first time about his intended departure in a few days. She is distraught. An emotional and dramatic happening often enacted *fuh true* in many Caribbean homes.

Now put these three scenes all together into one stage play, build a realistic set around it, rehearse the lines, movements and emotions, and understand the characters. Then perform the play on stage before a paying audience: you would be staging **Moon on a Rainbow Shawl** by Trinidadian playwright, Errol John! This play is and has been performed all over the Caribbean. In just those three short scenes of this full-length play, which is one of the set texts for the 1984 **CXC** English examination, you have calypso, storytelling, cricketing memories, family love, the power of authority, crime, boy-and-girl love betrayed, emigration,

and hopes for a better future. These are all part of real life, and all part of a staged play, and are interwoven to produce theatre in the Caribbean. The three real scenes could take you half a lifetime to see or experience; the stage shows you them in ninety minutes!

Theatre is everywhere, and everybody is involved in dramatic situations every day. When that real living moment is put into a formal package – a song, play, dance – then it becomes theatre of a different kind. It is now art. But it is still about us, and for us. It is still real, maybe it is now *more real* than usual. How could that be so? Why do people act on stage? What is the purpose of looking at life around us and acting it out in one way or another?

People make theatre for different reasons. A Caribbean dramatist described formal drama as **'the only way we can really examine our myriad clamouring selves'.** What do you think this description means? Why do you sing a song? Or write a poem? Why did your school choose a particular play to perform? Why do you jump up to calypso or a Carnival band, or sing and clap in time to a gospel song?

Perhaps you want to express the joy of life or to enjoy the feeling of group participation. Whatever the reasons, you are taking part in both the natural real living theatre of everyday life, and the staged theatre of performance. Each person takes part in staged theatre for different reasons, all of them useful to her or him.

Every culture, nation or people have always done some sort of special performances. Often it was for religious reasons, but whatever it was, it was needed for their welfare and peace of mind.

It is no different with today's staged perform-

1

The scene looks real, doesn't it? It is a scene from the stage play *Moon on a Rainbow Shawl* performed by the Theatre Guild more than 20 years ago in Guyana. The walls of the house are painted canvas, and the roof is cardboard. Is theatre true to life or is it all false?

ances of songs, dances or plays. Some people see a play as a mirror of life; some as a microscopic view of a tiny detail of living; some as an examination of different viewpoints. Some only come to enjoy wishful fantasy and to laugh. What other reasons are there? They are all valid; and theatre can fulfil them all. Theatre in the Caribbean is about us, our roots, traditions, our languages, our present problems, our dreams. Then what makes us so unique? What makes the theatre in the Caribbean different? Let us examine some of the differences and some of the similarities.

Exercises

There will be suggested activities after each chapter. They are meant to be used as ways of finding out more about theatre in the Caribbean. They may take the form of discussions, written responses, or activities. Each chapter poses several questions, and raises viewpoints which may lead to further discussion and research.

1. Have you ever seen a play with a scene in it that you have witnessed or experienced yourself in real life? Describe it.
2. What did you see or hear in the last 24 hours which might make a dramatic scene in a play? Could you tell the incident to your classmates? Act out as much of the story as you wish.
3. What other incidents in *Moon on a Rainbow Shawl* are true to life?
4. What calypsoes do you know which describe real incidents. Can you sing the whole calypso?

2 Speechifying and storytelling

Storytelling has always been an important part of people's lives in the Caribbean. Before radios were a part of daily life, and before most people could obtain or even read newspapers, the only way they found out about happenings in their country was by being told about them by somebody else. When village women took their fruits and vegetables to market in the city once a week, they brought back news and stories of what they had seen or heard. If a man's job carried him from village to village, he brought word of the local happenings he experienced on his rounds.

Myths, legends, and family histories were passed down from one generation to another as grandparents told father and mother, and parents retold the stories to their children. To impress their listeners and to keep their interest, the story tellers used many dramatic skills. They often used very colourful 'flowery' language, big words, rhymes and gestures to entertain their audience. This overall skill was known sometimes as 'speechifying'. Everybody has a certain amount of speechifying skill. There is at least one student in your classroom who is a good speechifyer.

Apart from telling stories, the art of speechifying has taken many other forms, all of them very entertaining, and some of them serving useful purposes. Many of the techniques have their origins or roots in both European and African cultures. Speechifying and storytelling, then, are some of the oldest dramatic arts in the Caribbean, and have helped to continue the culture of the region. Different forms have developed from island to island. What are some of the Caribbean styles?

Robber speech

Since the early 1900s a colourful character has appeared on the streets of Trinidad during Carnival. Dressed like a fantastic cowboy, all in black, with cape, boots, toy six-shooter and a huge sombrero topped with a skull, the Midnight Robber is an extravagant braggart. Spotting a likely 'victim' on the street, the Midnight Robber will stop blowing on the whistle, which is always part of his outfit, and launch into a loud and long speech that has come to be known as 'robber talk':

> I am the mightiest gladiator of the oriental skies, a buccaneer of the East and West, who will horrify your auspicious sensibilities with my exuberant affluence of preponderous speechifying until alas and alack, you deliver some pecuniary transaction into my presence as presents . . .

A robber speech is impressive as much for its sound as its sense, full of empty threats and loud boasting. Although the gun is a fake, and no real physical contact is made, most people will gladly pay the Midnight Robber a few coins as ransom to escape his attentions.

Extempo calypso

Extempo calypso is an entertaining technique used by calypsonians to make up clever rhyming verses on the spot. They may be poking good-natured fun at another calypso singer or a person in the audience. They can also comment on more serious subjects like politics, poverty or racial attitudes. In the words of an old Jamaican proverb, 'You tek bad someting mek laugh'. That is the calypsonian's art, and the best extempo artists can create spon-

3

taneous verses for an hour, never repeating themselves. Extempo is sometimes known as impro by calypsonians. Can you trace the origins of these words, and their meanings?

A calypsonian can put a listener on the spot by telling

Hey Mister, I like the shirt you wearing,
But the sleeve look like it tearing.
I know you say it very costly
But I think it come from the Salvation Army!

It's not always fun to be the object of a calypsonian's attentions. As 'Sparrow' Slinger Francisco, of Grenada and Trinidad, puts it in his calypso **Lulu**

Ah'm afraid you make a calypso o' me
Ah know nobody going see, an' is only
    the two o' we
Sparrow ah 'fraid you goin' make a
    calypso o' me.

Tea party

This is a Sunday social in Antigua. Participants are expected to give sermons on various themes from the Bible. They must use actual quotations and colourful biblical language, and must not pause to remember. Everyone joins in the singing of hymns during the Tea Party. Similar traditions exist in Jamaica, St Croix, Barbados and other territories. The Barbados version, called 'Service o' Song', may include extempo verses about incidents and people of the village.

Stick-fighting

As described in *Music in the Caribbean* — the first book in this series — stick-fighting, as seen in Trinidad and Tobago, is a dangerous but dramatic sport. It includes 'kalinda' drumming, dancing and the 'singing of scornful verses about the opponent and his family'. That is speechifying at its most dramatic. Trinidadian poet Victor D. Questel has used this particular tradition to write a poem about stick-fighting called **Man Dead**:

. . . Gall is my rum
Violence my chaser
I was the goat
which spawned the first drum.
I am the man who killed Cain
Given half a chance
I'll kill you again.

When performing his poem, it could be accompanied by all the environment of the stickfight, including the drumming, chanting, movements.

At an open-air museum theatre, two dancers of the Barbados Dance Theatre during a 'stick-lickin'' scene.

Folksongs

Traditional folksongs are good examples of how special incidents are remembered through music, and also provide excellent songs for more formal theatre plays.

In Guyana, there are many rivers and creeks with fast-running currents and very treacherous waterfalls. One of them is the Itanami. All of the boatmen were afraid of 'shooting the rapids' — rowing through the tumbling water and jutting rocks. Out of that frightening experience came one of the most popular and dramatic Guyanese folksongs.

One morning de captain wake,
De captain wake, he wake de boatman,
De boatman wake, he wake de bowman,

De bowman wake wid a paddle in he han',
'All I want is a long and strong,
Itanami is too much for me'.

When this folksong is performed nowadays, mime is used to dramatize the story. This form of story-song exists in all cultures, and it would be easy to identify similar songs from your own traditions.

Informal debates

In Woodford square in Trinidad's capital city of Port of Spain, you will often see circles of ten to twenty people (usually men) loudly debating the events of the day — politics, cricket, crime, religion, marriage. Two or three men in the centre of the group will lead the 'debate', but those on the outer circle will interject their comments at any time. They use most of the story-teller's and actor's skills of voice control, gestures, expressive language, timing.

Similar situations occur in all cities of the world — like the 'Speakers Corner' in Hyde Park in London — and these informal group-debates are a natural type of 'free-form' theatre, where the length, outcome and even the physical shape of the audience grouping differ to suit the situation. These audience participation styles are not often used by writers, producers, actors or directors in our more formal theatre. Why do you think this is so? What would be the problems and the advantages of using more audience involvement in the formal theatre?

Anancy stories

The spinning of **Nancy stories** is one of the oldest storytelling traditions in the Caribbean. You probably have heard or read at least one of them. Anancy, the trickster spider, is the hero of countless Ghanaian legends, and the mythical character travelled to the Caribbean with the West African slaves. What villager slaving in a cane-field wouldn't enjoy a story about a quick talking, clever trickster who could always outwit the planter or his overseer?

In these Anancy stories, the trickster usually takes the form of a spider. He is always small and weak, but uses his quickwitted mind and speechifying tricks to talk himself out of dangerous situations. These stories have been dramatized in plays, dances, poems and songs. Slaves in the Southern United States transformed Anancy into the tales of **Brer Rabbit** and High John de Conqueror. Whatever form the stories take, they always have a moral at the end.

Here are two verses of a poem called **Anancy Cricket** by Guyanese John Agard. He calls himself a *poetsonian* and teaches about Caribbean cultures in schools in England. Agard is as 'nimbly spindly' a storyteller as Anancy himself. Can you picture the gestures, movements and voice changes that would make this Anancy story come alive?

> Tiger going for a hit,
> Moving down de wicket,
> Is six or sticks,
> He ent taking no Anancy tricks.
>
> But Anancy nimbly spindly hand
> Spinning at a rate,
> Tossing de ball from hand to hand,
> And spider, as you know, got eight.

Childhood memories

All young people have interesting things happen to them almost every day. Some of these incidents are funny, but many are tense, and often very active. When you tell your friends about these happenings, without even realizing it, you will use some of the storytelling techniques we have already described.

One of the most dynamic storytellers in Caribbean theatre is Marc Matthews of Guyana, and he is at his best when telling of his childhood experiences. In his **Jumbie Picnic** he relates a tale of four boys catching crabs in a burial ground. In the excerpt following, notice how many strong images are described very quickly but clearly. Can you imagine the sounds and the action which would accompany this story? The boys have already caught the crabs:

We make fuh start dishing out de hot soup in de tin cups we all bring wid we when . . . 'Whooooo Awhooo Whoooo!' . . . Carlton throw de pot up in de air wid fright . . . 'O me mumma!' 'O Jezums is ghost!' 'O Gawd spirits!' 'Jumbie!' De hot soup fly up in de air and den fall pon Touchteeth Egbert. Small Boy go to run, but he foot an' he han' ent go togedduh, so he runnin, runnin, runnin, but he ent goin, nowhere . . .

In telling this story, a talented story teller like Marc Matthews uses his entire body to portray all the actions and sounds.

At the other end of the island chain, in Nassau, Bahamas, schoolteacher Pandora Gibson-Gomez uses memories of her religious upbringing in her work. Pandora is a comedienne and storyteller, with most of her stories coming from the comic things she experienced as a child.

We have seen how speechifying and story-telling are a day-to-day part of the theatrical scene in the Caribbean. Over the years many creative people have drawn on their own experiences, traditional speechifying techniques, everyday dialects, and familiar images to relate, explain and express the meanings of their lives. This oral tradition has helped to carry forward the culture of the Caribbean from one generation to the next. In the following chapter we will see how modern artists have used these roots to fashion more formal works for the theatre.

Exercises

You will notice that most of the exercises are very active. Theatre is a very active thing, and is best performed rather than talked about or written about. However, some of these exercises can be in the form of discussion or as a written exercise.

1. Write a robber speech and perform it. It need not be more than a minute long.
2. Can you extempo? First deliberately write out at least one verse about someone or something in the school. Remember to keep it harmless and fictitious. Now find an appropriate tune and sing it. A group of 10

Body language at its most expressive is one of the special skills of Marc Matthews. Not so long ago we were taught to do 'verse speaking' without using the hands or body — just the voice. Why has this changed?

students should be able to do all this in about 30 minutes. The next step would be for you to invent a verse on the spot.

3. Form a large circle with two of you in the centre. Mime having sticks in your hands. While those in the circle beat out a rhythm with hands and feet and voices, the two stickfighters have to create at least one dance step each; keep quickly changing the two in the centre until all have invented a step. Now put them all together in one complete dance.

4. You all know at least one folk song. In groups of four, choose a song for each group and act it out. Use any of the various performing art techniques you know.

5. Form a circle about eight feet in diameter. Debate or discuss any subject which arises from this chapter. Use the style described in informal debates. You may use the questions at the end of *Informal Debates* as subjects for discussion or debates.

6. Can you identify any of the traditions which are mentioned in this chapter as having appeared in any plays you have read or seen? They may appear in different forms, language, styles, so you will have to look very carefully.

7. Would you like to act out the short excerpt of *Jumbie Picnic*?

3 Poetry as drama

We have seen how the oral tradition of story-telling and speechifying has become part of daily life in the Caribbean. Yet when Caribbean children go to school they are taught that good poetry should mimic the language and style of the old time English poets. Can you identify some of these?

Fortunately, over the years, Caribbean poets began to notice that the people around them did not talk to each other in very proper, standard English. Instead, in the streets, schoolyards, and on the playing fields, they themselves talked and heard folks talking together in popular, colourful dialects.

This everyday language varies from country to country, and sometimes from district to district on the same island. Among some of the English-speaking territories, the dialects are known as 'creolese', and on the French islands, they are called 'patois'. The dialect used in Dutch-speaking Surinam is 'srnan tongo', and in the Netherland Antilles, 'papiemento'.

Most Caribbean children learn these dialects even before they go to school, from parents and friends, so sociologists call them 'first languages' or 'nation languages'. It is the language most people will use when they are very excited or annoyed, pleased or unhappy.

Some of today's Caribbean poets reasoned that the best way to describe in poetry their experiences and feelings about the Caribbean is in the dialect speech styles they heard every day all around them. They also were interested in the average person in the street as their 'audience' and not only the élite or very educated.

Louise Bennett

The one person who has been most influential in popularizing dialect poetry in the Caribbean is Louise Bennett of Jamaica. Fondly known by her radio name of 'Miss Lou', Louise Bennett has been writing and performing her own poetry since the 1940s. She is one of the first Caribbean performing artists to comment effectively about life in Jamaica in the first language of her own country.

Miss Lou studied acting at the Royal Academy of Dramatic Art in London. When she returned to Jamaica, through her radio programmes, she taught a whole generation of Jamaican children about folk songs, poems and Caribbean stories in their own dialect. Her use of her first language is both expressive and attractive, as can be seen in her poem **Cuss Cuss**, in which one quarrelling woman ridicules another's ugly feet. See how much more colourful the insult becomes in dialect?

> Yuh foot shapeless an lang
> Like smaddy stan far fling dem awn
> An meck dem heng awn wrang.

Would you be able to translate that into your own dialect or first language?

She also poked fun at those who use big words or very 'highclass' English just to impress others. In her **Dryfoot Bwoy**, she writes about a young man who returns to Jamaica after a short visit to England, and about his rejection of his first language.

> Wha wrong wid Mary dry-foot bwoy?
> Dem gal got him fe mock,
> An wen me meet him tarra night
> De bwoy gi me a shock!

The one and only Miss Lou performing her popular poetry. Most of the Caribbean islands have similar dress which we sometimes call 'national costume'. What do you think is the reason for the use of these costumes?

Me tell him say him auntie an
Him cousin dem sen 'howdy'
An ask him how him gettin' awn,
Him say 'Oh, jolly, jolly'!

Miss Lou performs her work dressed in colourful, traditional folk-costume, and her theatrical style and good humour are admired and applauded wherever she performs. Her strong acting skills also helped to develop the famous Jamaican Pantomime. You will read more about this in Chapter 7 on *Musical Theatre*.

Paul Keens-Douglas

One of the younger dialect poets who has been directly influenced by Louise Bennett is the Trinidadian Paul Keens-Douglas. He is very popular, and many people who have never seen him perform have heard his records played over the radio.

Paul Keens-Douglas uses several styles of writing, including comic, romantic, blank verse, narrative, and he sometimes performs with musical accompaniment. Like all performing dialect poets, his work is best seen and heard in performance, rather than quietly read. He first started writing and performing poetry when he was a student at the University of the West Indies in Jamaica where he also participated in plays. This theatre training has given him a well controlled voice, a sense of comic timing, and an expressive use of his entire body.

If you have not heard at least one of Paul Keens-Douglas's poems or stories, then you may be living in Belize, Turks, or the Cayman Islands, because those are the only English-speaking territories in which he has not performed.

Among his many creations is the flamboyant character of 'Tanti Merle' who is a strong-willed woman. She has become almost as well known as her creator. In his story **Tanti at the Oval**, she is in the stands at a historic and exciting cricket match between the Windward Islands and Trinidad and Tobago. Toward the end of the story, the last nine balls of the game are being bowled. Imagine the tension and excited sounds from the huge crowd of enthusiastic cricket fans in Queen's Park Oval, Port-of-Spain:

> Excitement in de Oval like yu never see in yu life,
> Gore come in to bat an' is den de action start.
> Nine balls seven runs to go . . . noise in de place.
> Eight balls seven runs to go . . . Tanti start wavin' de basket.
> Seven balls six runs to go . . . Tanti on top de seat.
> Six balls five runs to go . . . Tanti fall off de seat.
> Five balls five runs to go . . . Tanti wavin' de parasol.
> Four balls four runs to go . . . police cautionin' Tanti.
> Three balls three runs to go . . . Ah can't even see Tanti.
> Two balls three runs to go . . . Tanti climbin' over de fence
> One ball two runs to go . . . Tanti on de people field.
> Gore hit de ball, an' he an' Finlay pelt down de wicket for two run,
> An' is den bachanal start . . .

This action-filled poem will help to keep alive the memory of an exciting moment in the history of West Indian cricket. Dramatic writing is like an interesting history lesson and good poetry can immortalize incidents and people. Paul has written and published several books of poems and stories, and made at least five L.P. records of his work in performance.

Through the work of oral poets like Louise Bennett and Paul Keens-Douglas, there has been a growing acceptance of dialect as a valid

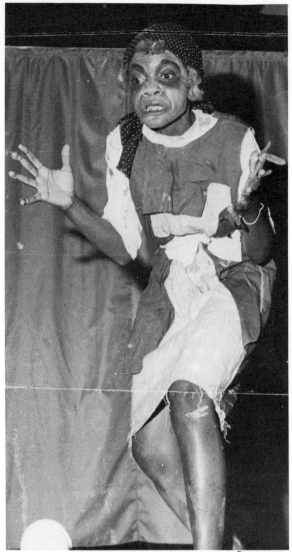

What did this schoolgirl do to become this hideous character? The legendary creature of the poem *Ol' Higue* by Guyanese poet Wordsworth McAndrew comes alive through the imagination and skill of this young interpreter, Grace Chapman. Ol' Higue could turn into a ball of fire and suck children's blood. Does your country have a similar character?

and powerful means of artistic expression. Public acceptance has made it possible for many performers to work in ways that were not acceptable 25 years ago. The styles of these modern **oral poets** and storytellers are very varied, but all are concerned with the political,

Poetry, story-telling, music and the three-man *All-Ah-We* team during one of their shows. They were a flexible group, capable of a one-man performance or a full concert with a ten-piece band. Standing from left to right: Ken Corsbie, Marc Matthews, Henry Muttoo.

social and economic welfare of the people of the Caribbean. Some of their tales are comic, some sad, some angry; while some depend on body language, costume and make-up for emphasis, others need only the intricate use of the voice. Some poets use music in different ways to underline and emphasise their messages and meanings. It is this creative and theatrical blending of various aspects of our culture which gives the modern poets an increasing popularity.

Calypsonians

Although the oral tradition survives in song and stories in all of the territories, perhaps its most striking and popular form developed in Trinidad and Tobago. Here the mixture of many national cultures have gone into the creation and development of the calypso. The infectious rhythms of the calypso suggest lighthearted fun, but the words of the song can make very serious comments about island life. There are some people who feel that calypsoes are the most important poetry of the Caribbean. Everybody sings or dances to calypsoes. Every year in the Caribbean there must be hundreds of new calypsoes created specially for the various carnivals and festivals.

Sometimes, calypsoes can become a dramatic historical record of real incidents. Nearly fifty years ago the German dirigible (motor-powered hot-air balloon), 'Graf Zeppelin' visited Trinidad and caused much excitement. Within a few months, a famous calypsonian known as Attilla the Hun had composed a song about it. Here is one verse:

One Sunday morning I chance to hear
A rumbling and a tumbling in the atmosphere,
I turned to stare, people flocking everywhere,
It was the Graf Zeppelin that had
Come to pay a visit to Trinidad.

Although that was many years ago, this song

11

helps to keep the memory alive. It was used in the Carnival play **Jouvert** in 1982.

In the weeks leading up to Carnival in most of the islands, different groups of calypsonians organize calypso tents and compete with each other to draw audiences. The entire atmosphere in these tents is that of very good theatre, as they have most of the elements that Caribbean audiences enjoy – music, mime, acting, speechifying by the Master of Ceremonies (the emmcee), extempo, dance, audience response, comedy, and some serious social comments too.

Today, many calypsonians use accompanying actors to act out the story as they sing, and they themselves may wear suitable costumes to fit the song they're singing. One of the more dramatic calypsonians is the Mighty Gabby of Barbados who uses his entire movements of his whole body to fully express his song. In his road-march winning tune **Jack** at the 1982 Crop-over Festival, he comments about the need for the Bajans to share at least equally the beaches with the many tourists. Every time he performs *Jack*, the audiences 'jump-up' and sing along with him.

> That beach is mine,
> I can bathe anytime
> Despite what they say
> I can bathe anywhere.

Despite the popularity of calypso, and its obvious dramatic storytelling qualities, there have been very few plays written in the Caribbean which are centered around this art form or about the lives of the calypsonians. Why do you think this is so?

Dub poets and reggae

Calysonians are not the only indigenous poets of the Caribbean who use folk traditions in their art. There are my oral poets who use heavy musical rhythms as a strong background for their work. American 'soul' and 'funk' singers have been using their own rhythmic background for their 'rap' or talk songs. Can you remember hearing them on your radio or from

The Mighty Gabby of Barbados, an extempo expert, made his living for years singing in night clubs. In full costume of a Barbadian soldier, he delights his audience singing his *Boots* in which he comments about the Defence Force. This song was banned by the radio stations in that island, and they would only play the 'version' or musical arrangement. *Boots* was one of the most popular calypsoes throughout the night clubs in the country. Why would radio stations ban a song?

jukeboxes? The Caribbean equivalents are the dub poets of Jamaica, who may have been influenced by their American counterparts. They use the true Jamaican roots rhythm of reggae as a pulsing background to their poetry. Why do you think they are called 'dub' poets?

These Jamaican rhythms and styles have influenced many Caribbean artists. The outstanding example in Barbados is performing poet Winston Farrell. He has been able to retain his natural Bajan dialect and accent in his work. The following is from one of his works, **Bus Man**:

> Every morning dem waiting
> By de bus stop

Dem talking bout
De Bus Man.
School children and workers
Baskets of huskers waiting for
De Bus Man.
Must be fun man
Driving dem bus man.
In dem streets man
Wid de Bus Man.
Backing down wid dem corners
Wheeling round dem bends
Sailing through dem cars and ting
Hear de engine sing
De Bus Man.

This poem can be performed with an audience echo – responding to the line 'De Bus Man' – and with a rhythmical handclapping or foot-tapping.

Of course you will have heard the great Bob Marley, reggae superstar. Do you know how reggae developed and from what roots? Unfortunately Bob Marley died in 1980, at the peak of his creative talents, but his influence on music remains. His songs have become the theme music for a whole generation of young people in the Caribbean and even in many other parts of the world. Why do you think he was so internationally popular?

He drew on the beliefs of the 50-year old Rastafarian religion, and his songs are of both celebration and protest. Drawing on the words of Psalm 137 he popularized the famous *Rivers of Babylon* which has been used many times with great emotional and dramatic effect in various stage productions throughout the Caribbean.

> By the rivers of Babylon,
> Where we sat down,
> And there we wait,
> When we remember Zion.

His imaginative use of biblical references and the danceable reggae beat made it world famous. Reggae has even influenced Trinidad's calypsoes in some cases. Is there an American equivalent of reggae music? Films and plays about Rastafarians have been produced. Do you know of any?

Picture a Rastafarian, with his long mane-like hair in 'dread locks', singing his songs. You probably have a photograph in a magazine at home. He is a powerful visual and emotional image on any stage. Among the many plays about him, was the musical **O Babylon** by St Lucia's playwright and poet, Derek Walcott. Have you heard of any other plays or poems about Rastafarians?

Barbadian rastafarian dub poet Winston Farrell blends the basic reggae 'riddims' with his Bajan tuk-band, and writes about Barbadian situations such as the scene at the bus terminal in Bridgetown. He is one of the younger artists of the Caribbean.

Influence of religion

Rastafarianism is not the only religion to influence our poets; in fact religion is a very common theme and focus for the arts. Because religion has always had a very strong influence on the lives of most Caribbean people, some poets and storytellers draw on their own religious backgrounds to develop their personal styles.

Have you ever stopped to listen to a street-corner preacher? Or attended a church service where the congregation responded to the preacher's sermon with clapping and cries of 'Amen' or 'Hallelujah'? Many dances have been choreographed using various religious ceremonies as their inspiration. Barbadian Tony Thompson wrote and directed an exciting play called *Fuzzy Sermon* with the theme, dialogue, music and songs taken from ceremonies of the Spiritual Baptist religion in that

One of the few plays written about a calypsonian, *Rum and Cocacola* depicted the cultural problems which face a Caribbean artist who has to make a living singing for the tourists. The playwright, Mustapha Matura of Trinidad, is a professional dramatist now living in England. The actors are Horace James and Learie Joseph. This publicity picture was posed on a Trinidad beach specially for the production at the Normandie Hotel Dinner Theatre.

island. The Tie-heads, as they are popularly known, use much clapping, swaying and call-and-response. Some pop singers and groups encourage their audiences to respond by clapping and chanting choruses.

Barbadian Bruce St John is a trained classical singer and a lecturer in Spanish literature at the University of the West Indies in Barbados. He is also a leading dialect poet. In his poem **Bajan Litany** he uses the call-and-response style of some church services to fully emphasize the theme. His audiences enjoy the involvement, and usually participate with enthusiasm.

Follow pattern kill Cadogan.	YES LORD.
America got black power?	O LORD.
We got black power too.	YES LORD.
Wuh sweeten goat mout bun 'e tail.	O LORD.
Bermuda got tourism?	YES LORD.
We got too.	O LORD.
De higher monkey go, do more he show 'e tail.	YES LORD.

Have you noticed another roots tradition used in this poem that we have not yet mentioned?

In the last chapter we showed how the memories of childhood have inspired story-tellers like Marc Matthews and Pandora Gibson-Gomez. Guyanese song-writer and leader of the band *The Tradewinds*, Dave Martins, also remembers his **boyhood days**, and sets them to poetry and song in calypso style.

Remember learning to ride a bike,
And learning how to cuss?
Drinking cocunut water in de country
Till yuh belly nearly bus'?
Hiding in de backyard smokin' a cigarette?
An' when dey give yuh castor-oil,
Yuh livin' in de toilet?

I remember still,
And I always will,
Time cannot erase
Boyhood days.

Can you add more verses of your own to this calypso?

Combined styles

Perhaps you have noticed that sometimes there is a mixture of more than one roots influence in a single poem or story. It would be possible to combine a wide range of these traditions and produce very dramatic theatre. Even the names of such mixtures have combined descriptions – 'action poems', 'song stories', 'choreosongs'. Whatever you choose to call them, they can all be exciting to perform.

One particular poet uses several styles in one poem. Perhaps he does it consciously, or it may be just a natural expression of his many influences. Abdul DeCoteau Malik, born in Grenada but living in Trinidad for many years, is an impressive looking performer of his own works. He is tall and strong, with a deep musical voice which compliments the tunes and rhythms he writes into his work. His **Revo** is such a poem.

Chorus: Never free, Never free, Never
           me.   (chant)
Narrator: Who beg fuh work shan't get,

And who ent beg don't want.
           (Caribbean proverb)
Chorus: Never free, Never free,
           Never me.
Narrator: I za limer
           labourer
           loose end
           writer
           limboing
           dis pole.
           Lancing . . .
Chorus: . . . pole!
Narrator: One more . . .
Chorus: . . . time!

(Call-and-response work-song of the men who raise the long heavy telephone poles in Trinidad & Tobago.)

Can you imagine how that could be performed with dancers, singers, actors and musicians?

Working with dialects, music, sound and voice, these modern poets have helped people in the Caribbean see themselves and their cultures in new, positive ways. The dramatic techniques which these poets use can be found in every culture. Can you think of examples of poems and stories and songs you have studied that have these same dramatic qualities?

Exercises

1. Perform a dialect poem of your own choice. If you need, request the assistance of your classmates.

2. Imitate Miss Lou's Jamaican dialect and perform one of her works.

3. Translate a dialect poem into standard English. Then reverse the process: take an English poem and put it in your first language. What effects do you get?

4. With fellow students as batsmen, fielders, spectators, and one as Tanti Merle, act out the last nine balls of that game. You will need a narrator or a chorus.

5. Dub poetry could be easy. With a background of reggae rhythm from your classmates, just tell of something in your own life. Even getting to school that morning could be interesting in this form.

4 Plays for everybody

Dramatic plays in the English-speaking Caribbean have been influenced by several cultures, and the history of the formation and development of such drama is about 300 years old.

Jamaica had a public theatre in 1682. Barbados had organized dramatics in 1729; George Washington, who became President of the USA, saw *The London Merchant* there in 1751. Antigua had its first theatre in 1788, and St Lucia in 1832. Theatre, however, was part of the cultural heritage of the ruling class, and plays performed in the 19th century said little or nothing about Caribbean life.

In 1897, Trinidad celebrated 100 years of British rule, and the occasion was marked with the first full-length West Indian historical drama we know of. *Carmelita, the Belle of San Jose* was written by Lewis Osborn Innis, is set in Trinidad and tells the story of the love of a Spanish-Indian girl named Carmelita for a young Englishman, Frank Norton. It is interesting to note that, although 80% of the island's population was black, that group is not represented in this early historical drama.

Nearly all the full-length plays which were staged in the 19th century originated in England. They were written by English people, some of whom were living and working in the Caribbean. It was only in this century that coloured people began to take part in these plays, but when they first started they usually played European characters, and sometimes put on make-up in order to look white. The language was 'proper' or standard English, usually of the type known as Oxbridge, which is an accent originating in England usually used by people educated at certain élite schools or universities.

In the 1930s, a famous black man called Marcus Garvey was spreading the idea that all black people in America and the Caribbean should investigate and re-adopt their lost African cultures and traditions. These would include their music, songs, dances, drama and religions.

Garvey was deported from the United States to Jamaica in 1927. In the early 1930s, his United Negro Improvement Associated established an open-air stage at Edelweiss Park in Kingston. He wrote and produced three plays which mark a turning point in Caribbean theatre. For the first time, a black man was presented on stage in the West Indies as a dignified, intelligent human being. On stage at Edelweiss Park, black actors could practise and develop their formal theatre skills.

It was also from the 1930s that the Caribbean people began to become more conscious of politics, and the possibility of national independence.

From that time, the Caribbean theatre has changed very much. More people became interested in the arts, and they began to look for ways of expressing their lives in more realistic language, characters and situations. They were inspired to make stage dances and presentations out of their own folksongs and religious festivals. They began to write poetry about real incidents, and in the languages they used naturally, their first languages. They began to paint scenes and people they saw every day. Nowadays, all new Caribbean plays, dances songs and paintings reflect today's people, happenings, ideas and everday life and longings.

There are, however, still some drama groups which produce good plays written in North America. England and Europe. There are many groups which only produce locally written plays; and there are groups which do mainly regional plays. Different groups perform their plays in different ways and for different reasons.

Drama groups

In every territory in the Caribbean, there is at least one drama group or club which continues to specialize in producing plays which they think their audiences will enjoy. The Theatre Guild of Guyana, which started 28 years ago, has its own theatre (The Playhouse), and continues today to produce a wide variety of good plays. The Little Theatre Movement (LTM) of Jamaica has produced the famous Jamaican Pantomime for forty years! The Trinidad Theatre Workshop and the Strolling Players have both been active for at least twenty years. In Barbados, the Greenroom players have produced foreign plays since the 1930s, and only recently have begun to include Caribbean plays. The Courtyard Players of St Croix have produced dozens of excellent international plays since their formation in 1967, and they have also staged many Caribbean plays including three written in St Croix.

The little island of Nevis has its Drama and Cultural Society (NEDACS), which organizes an annual festival of cultural events, including a Caribbean play. Bahamas has the Drama Circle which has been active for two decades. The Cayman Drama Society started in 1969 and is still producing at least two plays a year, of American or European origin. Can you name the drama groups in your country? Don't forget the drama club in your school. Would you like to see more drama groups producing more plays? Why do you think there are not too many drama productions in your country?

Foreign plays

As expected, most of the plays produced in the first half of this century were those which had already proven their worth in England, America or Europe. Among them were the English 'classics' written by Shakespeare, Noel

One of the most famous of Shakespeare's plays, *Hamlet*, being performed by a mixed cast of actors in Guyana. Can you spot the four racial groups here?

A typical English play performed in the Caribbean, in which the European and North American residents of the islands excelled. The language, dress, mannerisms and situations came naturally to them. The play is *When We Are Married* by J. B. Priestley – a Greenroom Players production.

Coward, George Bernard Shaw and many others. There were also a wide variety of plays by famous American playwrights like Tennessee Williams and Eugene O'Neill. From about 1960, we began to see plays written by Afro-Americans which were specially designed to show the social and political conditions of the black people in that country. Among the best known of them was *Raisin in the Sun* by Lorraine Hansberry. About that time too, Caribbean drama groups discovered African plays by Wole Soyinka, and more recently by the South African Athol Fugard. You may not have heard of many of these great playwrights.

Caribbean drama groups also produced popular Russian, German and French plays which had been translated into English. Occasionally, and only in Guyana or Trinidad, you may see a play written in India and produced by local groups made up of Asian-Caribbeans. These are usually historic or religious classical

plays, and always include several dances and songs.

When the best foreign plays are staged and acted well they are positive additions to our understanding of those societies, and of the art of the theatre. The best international plays have themes about the human condition which are universal, and they can teach us something worthwhile, no matter what our backgrounds.

Folk and community theatre

There are many cultural organizations which form part of a village or community, and produce a variety of theatrical shows. These productions are often made up of many short items such as dances, songs and dramatic skits. These groups were formed to fill the need of the community – to express their particular ways of life in artistic terms. Occasionally they produce short plays made up by one of their

Although *Raisin in the Sun* was written by black American Lorraine Hansberry, it is always emotionally moving to Caribbean audiences today. Do you know what those real-looking walls could be made of? Have you ever gone backstage of a theatre and seen how they make their 'flats'? You too can make them in your carpentry classes in school. This is another Theatre Guild production in Guyana.

members or created by the entire group. The stories are often from actual incidents in their village or community. These short plays are easily understood by their audiences, and are usually comedies in the dialect of that community.

These organizations sometimes get assistance from Caribbean governments who try to encourage them to develop and produce their work. Such cultural groups are often considered to be vital to the cultural and social development of the nation. In Trinidad and Tobago, there is a big annual festival called *Best Village*, at which most of the village communities in these two islands take part in a variety of arts and crafts. They are encouraged to create and perform works which reflect the cultures and traditions and living of their particular community.

Among these drama groups, whatever type of plays they are doing, there must be thousands of people involved. Each person takes part for different reasons. What do you think are some of these reasons?

Amateurs and professionals

When an amateur theatre group gets together and decides to put on a play, they need money for many things including costumes, make-up and scenery. Sometimes they get donations from business people in the community. Sometimes they charge admission to their performances to help cover expenses. No one involved in such a production expects to earn any money from them.

In the Caribbean, drama originated and was developed mainly by amateurs — people who loved the theatre and did it for their own feeling of self achievement, improvement and entertainment. Today there are still very many more amateurs than professionals in the production of drama.

In professional theatre, plays are put on for a

19

profit. And for that, you must have audiences. There must be enough people who want to see a play, and those people must have enough money to be able to buy tickets. The people taking part depend to varying extents on making money from this work, just as any other worker in non-artistic jobs do. However, very few theatre people are able to make living wages from the theatre, but some have '8 to 4' jobs while acting professionally in the evenings. These are called semi-professionals. Do you know any professionals or semi-professional theatre people?

An increase in professional theatre people is most seen in Jamaica, where there may be several plays being performed at the same time in the five or six theatres in Kingston. Among

Odale's Choice is a unique example of sharing – from ancient Greece to present Caribbean, covering 2000 years and many cultures. Written by Ed. Kamau Brathwaite of Barbados, adapted from the Greek play *Antigone*, this version was re-set in Nigeria and used standard and dialect English. The actor on the left playing the King is Ron Robinson, who runs The Theatre Company, a professional drama group in Guyana.

the artistic and commercially successful full-time professional dramatists in the Caribbean are Paul Keens-Douglas, Louise Bennett, Trevor Rhone, Derek Walcott, and Dennis Scott (who is director of the Jamaica School of Drama and a poet and playwright/director). You will read more of Rhone and Walcott in later chapters. Perhaps you have heard too of Calvin Lockhart, the film actor from the Bahamas? There are others of course.

One thing is certain, the more there are of these full-time practitioners in the Caribbean, the more and better theatre there will be. Already there are some technicians who are making theatre their only profession and therefore taking the task much more seriously. The fact is that producing theatre is a highly complicated and commercial venture requiring a vast variety of skills and much dedication.

Producing a play

One of the reasons why there may not be as much theatre and drama as we would like to see is that producing a play is never an easy thing to do. Some drama groups try to produce their plays very elaborately, while others keep their productions as simple as possible. The more elaborate the production, the more complex and expensive all the arrangements can become. Here are just a few of the necessary things to be done in order to produce a play successfully:

- choosing the play;
- choosing the actors;
- finding the money for production;
- designing and constructing the scenery;
- arranging the lights and the operators;
- promoting the play to get the audiences;
- selling the tickets.

One of the most important production jobs is the promotion of the play. In the Caribbean it is one of the weaker areas among producers. Good advertising is usually a skilful but expensive task, and many groups depend entirely on the goodwill of the local newspapers and radio station for free publicity. Advertising has to be as carefully planned and carried out as the

The technical preparation for a play is sometimes as arduous and difficult as the acting. Caribbean theatre practitioners often have to be jack-of-all-trades – here are two of St Lucia's best dancers, Michael Francis and Carlton Ishmael, setting up the lights for a drama production in the Town Hall, Castries. See Chapter 7 on Musical Theatre.

actors having to learn their lines. Without audiences there will be no income for the producers to pay the expenses and to plan for further plays. Without audiences there can be no theatre, and the actors will have no reason to work that hard. Theatre is a communal art, because it depends on people performing and more people watching. It can only work well if many audiences pay for, and enjoy the plays.

Although good theatre depends on good performers to make it enjoyable for audiences, there are many other factors which are necessary. The physical and technical facilities have to be efficient to show off the actors at their best. The lighting and sound equipment have to be adequate and in good working condition. Unfortunately, in the Caribbean this technical

side of theatre has been slow in catching up to professional standards. There is even a great shortage of people trained to operate efficiently the equipment. Most of the stages in schools, community halls, and even in the theatres are not constructed or maintained in the most effective condition. Have you ever been to a play, a variety concert or a calypso tent and not been able to hear the performers too well? Or found that the seat you are in is blocked by the person in the seat in front of you, and you cannot see the stage properly? What other physical or technical things have gone wrong at shows you have attended? What are the necessary factors which will help to make theatre most enjoyable?

Unfortunately too, few theatre buildings in the Caribbean have been constructed particularly with drama in mind. But among the few well designed and equipped theatres are the Little Theatre in Kingston, Dundas Civic Centre in Nassau, Little Carib in Port-of-Spain, the Playhouse in Georgetown, and Queens Park in Bridgetown.

Theatres

Most theatre buildings in the region have their stages at one end of the auditorium, and all the audience watch the performance from one direction. There is usually a curtain which opens to reveal the actors playing in front of the scenery. This type of stage is called *Proscenium*, a strange name, but maybe you can

Is there anyone in your school who could design, build and dress a set like this one which Alwin Bully created for his mystery play *Nite Box*? See chapter 5 on Plays, Players and Playwrights.

The Little Carib set up for a centrally staged play, as seen from the balcony. It is possible to see this play four times and get four different views of the same play; everybody involved must be aware of that potential. Can you name at least six details of staging which must be considered?

trace its origins and its meanings by asking any theatre enthusiast, or looking for it in an encyclopedia in your library.

The reason for the popularity of this type of stage is because of the English tradition which started formal theatre in the Caribbean. Most plays in England during the 19th century were performed on proscenium stages. The majority of English theatres still continue to favour this form of stage, and the Caribbean's theatres are no different. But have you noticed that in real life, in everyday living experiences, we are not often arranged naturally in this way?

Up to the end of 1983, the only three Caribbean theatres which are set up very differently to the proscenium stages, are Little Carib (Trinidad), Steel Shed (Barbados) and Dorsch Center (St Croix). They all break the tradition and use flexible staging arrangements.

Little Carib is the most progressive theatre space, because it can be effectively used as a thrust, in-the-round, open-end, free-form and proscenium stage. Do these names help you to imagine what kind of stages these are?

Little Carib is also well raked all around to permit the audience good sightlines, no matter what stage form is used. You will never find your view of the actors blocked by the person sitting in front of you. This imaginatively designed theatre has also developed an elaborate home-made lighting system to suit the various changes. The technician, Francis Lewis, designed the system using garden spots and floodlamps, and household dimmers.

Dorsch Center in Fredericksted, St Croix is an open-air theatre which permits several staging arrangements. Do you know of any other open-air theatres? What would be the advantages and problems of such a theatre in your country? Remember that many of our plays are set in outdoor situations.

The smallest theatre is probably the Barn in Kingston, Jamaica, which has a tiny end-stage and seats only 150. The Barn is a very important theatre. It ran the historic **Smile Orange** play by Trevor Rhone, which was the first really long running play in the Caribbean, and a turning point in Jamaica's theatre history. The Barn was originally a small warehouse, but with imagination and much skill and dedication, it has been converted into one of the truly productive theatres in the region.

Can you think of any places or buildings which can be converted into a theatre? What changes and facilities would you need to make it an efficient production space? How would you go about making your school hall or auditorium or gymnasium into an effective theatre?

Drama in schools

Some people believe that one of the reasons Caribbean cricketers are so many and so good is because the game is played in primary and secondary schools. Would the same be true of the performing artists if all the theatre arts were encouraged and performed in the Caribbean schools? Most educators, including teachers, school principals, and government ministries agree that drama, dance, music and singing should be part of every child's education. Are these skills taught as a regular part of your school's syllabus? How much encouragement and facilities are given to you?

Jamaica, however, is an exception among the Caribbean territories, because of the interest and actions taken there to develop theatre in schools. There is a Cultural Training Centre with separate schools for art, music, dance and drama. The drama students there

What is unusual about this theatre? It's in the Steel Shed in Bridgetown, Barbados. The play is another production of *Moon on a Rainbow Shawl*, this time it is 1983, and the producer is Stage One, with the designer/director, Michael Gilkes.

are trained to become qualified teachers of drama in primary and high schools. This culturally-rich island also has a theatre programme in its University campus at Mona, with its own theatre which is managed by Noel Vaz.

In 1979 the governments of the Caribbean replaced the GCE (General Certificate of Education) which was set in England, with the regionally oriented CXC examinations. Since then there have been many changes in the content of the syllabus. Although the drama texts now show only two Caribbean plays out of nine set for the 1984 syllabus, there is a recommended additional reading list of 35 Caribbean plays. Most of these have been published by the Extra Mural Department of the UWI in Trinidad since the 1950s and early 1960s, but there is still a problem in obtaining these scripts.

Whatever playscripts are studied in schools, there are few staged productions of any of them. What benefits would be obtained by actual performance? What would your school need to produce plays which are on the CXC set text list?

Drama can teach skills as varied as voice control, acting, carpentry and teamwork. There are many other skills which can be learned from a good theatre arts programme in schools; can you name at least eight more? Drama can also be great fun while you learn. How and what should be the theatre arts programme in your school? Can you encourage your teachers to hold a series of discussions on these subjects?

If all the schools had a full programme of theatre arts as part of their everyday curriculum, then perhaps, the Caribbean would have theatre for *everybody*.

Exercises

1. Make a list of all the drama or cultural groups in your country. Include a brief description of their purpose, history, work and plans for

the future. Also include your own assessment of the quality of the groups.

2. What overseas plays have you seen, or heard on the radio or seen on TV? Have you read one either to yourself or as a group? Which moved you the most, and why?

3. Everybody has seen a short skit which they liked. Describe it or act it out.

4. Would you like to work in theatre? Describe what kind of work, why, and how you would do it.

5. Complete the list of production tasks involved in staging a play. There must be at least eight more necessary jobs to be done. Give a short description of each of them.

6. Work out a complete promotion plan for a play or concert your school may be doing next term. You want to attract audiences for sell-outs of at least three performances.

7. First sketch the various ways that your classroom could be rearranged for teaching, then move the desks and chairs around in all of the shapes. What are the differences of methods and types of teaching for each arrangement? Please do all this quietly.

8. Find three places outside the actual school building where you would put on a show, or play, or concert. How would you arrange the various facilities for effective theatre?

Drama in a high school gymnasium in Guyana. What are the particular features of this design by Henry Muttoo, who now teaches theatre design at the Jamaican School of Drama? Can your school do something like this? How and with what is the lighting system made?

5 Plays, players and playwrights

During the last 50 years there have been maybe thousands of plays written by hundreds of playwrights, and acted by countless players. Some of those plays may have been only fifteen minutes long, some had just two characters, others were very lavish and expensive productions. Many of the authors only wrote one play which had just one brief performance during a variety concert for a village or school community.

In every village, school, church group, drama group, and on all the radio and television stations, there have been talented men, women and children who have learnt lines, rehearsed their movements and performed in good and bad plays throughout the Caribbean. Trinidad dramatist Dr Errol Hill, who wrote the book **The Trinidad Carnival: Mandate for a National Theatre**, has spent many years collecting data about the plays written and produced throughout the Caribbean.

During the relatively short history of Caribbeanized theatre, there have been plays, players and playwrights that stand out for one reason or another. It is hoped that the following brief descriptions of a few of the important ones will encourage you to make your own research into Caribbean drama. Maybe you have seen one of the plays mentioned here or heard of an author or actor. Has your school studied or read any of them? Remember, however, that a written play is like written music; it has to be performed to be fully appreciated.

Most of the best Caribbean plays of the past thirty years have been concerned with examining the many aspects of daily living. They all use the first language of their characters. During the 1950s and 1960s, the plays which were mostly produced in the Caribbean were those which only had one act and used a single set.

These were easier and cheaper to organize than a full-length play; they normally only ran for 30–60 minutes on stage. Many of them were printed by the **Extra Mural Dept** of UWI in Trinidad. A few copies of some of these can still be found in school libraries, and some of the better ones continue to be produced occasionally. The CXC syllabus includes many of them in its recommended reading list.

At the same time that these plays were being published, two men travelled throughout the Caribbean encouraging people to form drama groups, and to perform Caribbean plays. They were Errol Hill and Noel Vaz who both worked for the Extra Mural Department, directed plays, lectured and demonstrated the vitality and relevance of these plays. Many people who first discovered an interest in theatre at that time are still very active in modern drama productions.

Plays

Not all of those short plays were comedies, but their writers knew that Caribbean audiences like to laugh, so even in their serious plays, they often created characters or situations which were humorous. **Ping Pong** by Errol Hill was such a play. In it a group of steelband players are preparing for an important competition, when one of them notices that the vital first pan has been damaged by an unknown rival. It is a play full of action, colourful Trinidadian first language, and is simple to stage.

But it is the full-length plays which attract the most attention. Well-established drama groups still produce *Moon on a Rainbow Shawl* in two long acts, with an elaborate single set, and a wide range of interesting characters. It was written by Errol John of Trinidad in 1957, when it won first prize in the *Observer* (a Sunday newspaper) play competition in Britain. It is now included as part of the CXC syllabus for high school study, and has been produced with great success as recently as 1983 by the Stage One group of Barbados.

Although the story is set in Trinidad in the late 1940s, *Moon on a Rainbow Shawl* continues today to be relevant to all of the Caribbean territories. One of its main characters is a poor tramcar driver who decides to leave his backyard ghetto, and try his luck in England. In all Caribbean territories today there is a constant flow of people leaving for America, Canada and England searching for improved living conditions.

In every territory there is usually at least one play which has had an important influence on the recent history of drama. It may be a particularly serious play which comments on the local political situation. In Montserrat such a play was **Son of a Bitch** by David Edgecombe; and in Dominica it was **Speak Brother Speak**, created by Danny Caudeiron and Alwin Bully especially for Carifesta '72 in Guyana.

In Jamaica it was a comedy which was the turning point for fully commercial drama in that island. *Smile Orange* by Trevor Rhone opened in 1971 and ran for 245 performances! It has most of the ingredients for good Carib-
bean theatre – action, imaginative and colourful language, comic situations, recognizable characters, and also includes critical comments about the society. The scene is set in a small tourist hotel in Jamaica, and the interaction between tourists and locals there. It was eventually made into a movie, which has been seen throughout the Caribbean.

Down the chain of islands in Trinidad, there was also a tremendously popular and successful comedy written by Freddie Kissoon, another schoolteacher. (Trevor Rhone is a qualified teacher.) **Calabash Alley** was written as a long serial for radio, and ran for a year before it was produced as a stage play. Many radio stations in the Caribbean ran the serial, and Kissoon's production group, the Strolling Players, then toured several islands with the stage version. That was during the 1960s, and your parents may have heard or seen it. If they did, would you ask them why they thought it was so popular? Are there similar radio serials or soap operas in your country?

There is an active theatre group called the Inn Theatre run by Geoff Creswell, a talented Englishman living in the Cayman Islands. Among the many plays Geoff has directed was

The shape of a theatre could influence the design of the set and the flow of the action. What kinds of stages are used for these two productions of *Pantomime*? The left is by Stage One in Barbados; the right by the All-Trinidad Theatre.

26

Time Longer dan Rope, the first full-length Caymanian play, and it was written by Frank McField in 1980. It was very critical of some of the social and political aspects of the Caymans, but was a turning point for the Inn Theatre, which followed it with several more Caribbean plays. Among them was Edgecombe's *Son of a Bitch* which was retitled *Sunova* for the Caymanian production. Why do you think this was necessary?

Derek Walcott's **Pantomime** is an important play for the Caribbean because, among other things, it fully exploited the quick-witted language of Trinidadians, is a two-man play and therefore not too difficult to produce, is both very funny and serious, and is about the problem of foreign versus local values and cultures. You all know the story of Robinson Crusoe and Man Friday, which is supposed to have taken place in Tobago? Well *Pantomime* is a modern-day version of the Crusoe/Friday story. The owner of a run-down hotel in Tobago is an Englishman who is trying to persuade his head-waiter to act in a short pantomime-like play about these two legendary characters. He is hoping to be able to entertain his guests with this comedy. Like most good comedies anywhere, this play, while very funny, also takes a hard look at many serious aspects of the culture of the Caribbean. It is a popular choice by theatres in and outside of the Caribbean where it has been produced in Trinidad, Barbados, Cayman Islands, Dominica and Jamaica.

Players

Caribbean people are natural actors. The historical backgrounds of the islands with their mixtures of strong folk cultures and traditions, have blessed us with very expressive dialects and body languages. We move easily, our music is varied and exciting, our environment is interesting, our politics are going through great changes, our religions are many, our racial mixtures and our skin colours of infinite variety.

But natural talent and exciting roots are not enough to make excellent actors. It takes a good deal of hard work, intelligence and discipline to master the many techniques which are needed fully to control those natural talents. We are fortunate that there are many Caribbean actors who have mastered the necessary skills. Perhaps you have enjoyed seeing a particular actor perform in a play at your school, or on television. Is there a student in your school who can always tell a good story? Are you a good actor yourself? What techniques do you think are needed to be a good actor? Do you know any of your friends who have some of those skills? Perhaps they too will make top-class Caribbean actors some day.

Each good actor has many talents, but there is usually at least one particular quality which stands out. When you think of a powerful voice, you may think of Errol Jones of Trinidad. Good comic timing? Well Wilbert Holder also of Trinidad has that in abundance. Which woman has both physical and personality power and vitality? You'd have to see Pandora Gibson-Gomez; while a natural warmth radiates from Charles Hyatt of Jamaica; and for attention-getting stage presence and wit, you would choose Louise Bennett. Tall handsome, athletic physique is Albert Laveau's strength. He is the Trinidad actor who worked as a fulltime professional for two years in the USA. As a bird is alert and quick, so too is Carl Bradshaw the Jamaican who created the role of the headwaiter in *Smile Orange*; and as a dangerous animal is alert and therefore you dare not take your eyes from him, so too does Marc Matthews have that quality. Bahamian lawyer Winston Saunders is an intelligently sensitive performer, and Leonie Forbes of Jamaica is noted for her sincerity. In Trinidad, Joy Ryan is just beautiful to watch in any role, even as the vulgar Jab Jab; while it would be difficult to find someone as unpredictably fluid in wit and with such a spontaneous sense of humour as Horace James, the television director.

All of these actors have varying mixtures of all the qualities which make up an entertainer's art. You can draw up your own list of talents displayed by the actors you have seen. Each island has its outstanding actors who entertain their audiences every time they perform.

Powerhouse actor, Errol Jones of Trinidad, during a rehearsal. If he were your teacher, imagine what would make him point at you like that.

Playwrights

Most dramatic productions depend on access to interesting playscripts, and the playwright is therefore very important to the development of good theatre. The Caribbean is lucky to have many talented writers who supply such scripts. However, your problem might be to find copies of those scripts when you wish.

Just as our musicians, calypsonians and actors have different styles, so too our good playwrights all have different approaches to their material. Some concentrate on comedies, some on highly political issues, while other mix these two elements. There is, too, a growing interest in musical plays about which you will read more in Chapter 7.

Many writers are leaders of drama groups. This assures that they have the means of getting their plays produced. Freddie Kissoon of Trinidad founded the Strolling Players, who have performed his works all over Trinidad and Tobago and in many other islands for the past twenty-five years! Kissoon has written 47 plays, with his radio serial *Calabash Alley* having 78 episodes. He also wrote most of the script for the Trinidad feature film *The Right and the Wrong*. To continue with this remarkable record, the Strolling Players have staged a total of more than 700 performances of 50 different plays. No other Caribbean writer or drama group can claim anything near these figures.

Kissoon's plays are always in dialect, usually very simple to follow, and contain a good deal of action and humour. What would you say is the value of such a group in an island? Have you heard of Freddie Kissoon and his Strolling Players before? Can you get copies of his playscripts at your local library or bookshops? Is there a need for a Caribbean publishing house for such books? Are Kissoon's plays only of interest in Trinidad? Maybe when drama becomes a necessary curriculum subject in our schools, there will be official action to ensure publication and distribution of our plays. Whatever the reasons, Kissoon's and other writers' scripts are not easily available to anyone interested in Caribbean theatre.

As a prolific writer/director of his drama group, Kissoon has his Guyanese counterpart in Francis Quamina Farrier and the Dramatic Core. Francis wrote two long radio serials and about 25 plays which the group performed all over the country districts of Guyana; that was during the 1960s and early 1970s. Farrier's style and theme were a bit more varied than Kissoon's, but were also deeply rooted in the traditions and history of his country.

It is clear from all of this that there is often one particular playwright in each island who is responsible for regular production of plays. These key people, together with fellow dramatists and other hardworking members, keep the theatre alive and active. In Antigua it is Dorbrene 'Fats' Omarde with his serious, politically concerned plays. In St Vincent, the New Artists' Movement (NAM) perform the works of Cecil 'Blazer' Williams; while in St Kitts nearly everyone has seen one of the plays of Clement 'Bouncin' Williams.

Apart from the islands of Montserrat, St Kitts, Nevis and Antigua, where the main drama groups occasionally arrange inter-island tours of plays, there is very little exchange of productions from one island to another. There is no system of regular inter-island production, so that development on each island tends to be isolated. What do you consider to be the main reasons for this lack of communication? What benefits, if any, would be derived from more drama groups touring and exchanging their skills? Chapter 9 discusses this idea of sharing more thoroughly.

In Dominica, the outstanding dramatist is Alwin Bully. Like nearly all the playwrights of the Caribbean, he is director and producer of his own plays. He helped form the Peoples' Action Theatre (PAT) in the early 1970s, and it is the only theatre group which produces regularly. Bully is a versatile writer: two musicals, a murder mystery called **Nite Box**, two radio serials, and an epic play about the disastrous volcano which hit Martinique in 1903 called **Pelée**.

The chapter on musical theatre will explain his musical plays more fully, but let's look briefly at another aspect of theatre which we can demonstrate through Alwin Bully's writing. He has often demonstrated the positive power of drama. After Hurricane David struck Dominica in 1979, destroying or damaging most of the agriculture and homes on that island, he wrote and directed a series of local radio drama. It was designed to encourage and educate the dispirited people to think and work positively towards rebuilding their morale and their homes again. With radio being the only sure means of communication for many people, his serial was of special importance to listeners who needed the encouragement to work towards rebuilding their houses, roads and farms. It is interesting to note here that Alwin Bully was once the headmaster of Dominica's major secondary school.

Is there some connection between dramatists and schoolteaching? Are there any teachers in your school also deeply involved in theatre? Another example of this connection is one of Trinidad's top calypsonians, the Mighty Chalkdust, who lectures at the UWI in Trinidad, and teaches Social Studies at Mucurapo Senior High School in Port-of-Spain.

Another playwright whose name has become almost a household word in his country is David Edgecombe of Montserrat. His plays have often toured Antigua and St Kitts. His *Kirnon's Kingdom* (see page **58**) has also been produced in the Cayman islands, St Croix, and Barbados.

St Lucia was very fortunate to have been birthplace and home to the Walcott twins – Roderick and Derek. These two remarkable men were writing and directing their own plays there as early as the 1950s. Today they are still very productive. Unfortunately for the Caribbean, Roderick now lives in Canada. Derek is one of the most versatile and prolific Caribbean playwrights, creating about thirty plays in as many years. He is also an internationally recognized poet. Have you heard of any other playwright anywhere in the world who has written musicals, historical drama, two-character plays, comedies, tragedies, epics, in both standard and dialect English and in patois? Six of Derek Walcott's plays are included in the 1984 CXC recommended reading list.

The Walcott twins often used many of the Caribbean traditions as themes. Roderick wrote about the La Rose Festival in three of his works, and a speechifying street preacher in **The Harrowing of Benjy**. Derek filled his **Ti-Jean and His Brothers** with myths and patois folk songs. His **Marie La Veau** musical uses voodoo as a central image, while his **In a Fine Castle** is about a fading French Creole family in Port-of-Spain. His **Charlatan** is about a calypsonian and fake obeah man. *Dream on Monkey Mountain* stresses African memories and cultures.

You may have heard of plays in America or England which have run for many years. *The Mousetrap* has been running in London for 25

Alwin Bully conducting a workshop at the Jamaica School of Drama. He was the headmaster of a high school on the island, and he is a Caribbean dramatist with many skills. What are some of those skills necessary for a productive, successful theatre person in the region?

staged. Occasionally, the actors and director create the play by discussion, and improvization. Little children improvize stories on the spot all the time. Have you ever seen some six year olds 'making up' stories? They do not need to have an audience, as they create a play for their own enjoyment. You must have done that yourselves a few years ago.

Improvization is an accepted method by a few dramatists and directors to help create a play or sometimes just a scene. Extempo calypso is based on the same principle.

Many years ago, Errol Hill and participants at a drama workshop in Jamaica created a play called **Sleepy Valley** by just such improvization. Only afterwards did they write out the script. The main characters are Blue Mountain, Big River and Little Foothills who are angry with the lazy villagers for not improving their living conditions. *Sleepy Valley* was on the CXC syllabus for 1983.

Occasionally, playwrights have written about schools in major plays. Another school-teacher playwright, Anthony Hinkson, who is one of the very few full-time drama teachers in Caribbean schools, wrote **Teacher Teach'er**. It was a play which was very critical of the education system in Barbados. The Jamaican school system came in for severe criticism from Trevor Rhone in his *Schools Out*, which was also a popular hit with audiences. The Barbados Festival Choir's musical play *Bimshire '83* was about the effect of the 'Eleven Plus' examinations which young people have to take to qualify for the better high-schools.

How many of the CXC syllabus plays have you read? Do you sometimes wish plays were performed more often in your school, instead of only reading them in a classroom book? Remember that you yourselves can improvize and produce a play. Your interest in theatre is a first step towards encouraging school teachers and administrators to include more drama in school activities.

years, while *The Fantasticks* has been showing in New York for 20 years! Perhaps the record in your island has been 21 performances? Well **Old Story Time** ran for 287 performances in Jamaica! That is a very long time in the Caribbean. It was written by Trevor Rhone who had also created the record-breaking play of *Smile Orange*.

Old Story Time is about changes and conflicts in the society when the old traditional native way of life clashes with the modern European or American cultures. It is a play both comic and tragic, but with an ending that gives hope for the future. It ends with a very dramatic obeah scene which suggests that our hope for a better future lies in holding on to some of our traditional folk values. Caribbean audiences were lucky to see this play during Carifesta '81 in Barbados, with the two great Jamaican actors Leonie Forbes and Charles Hyatt performing in it.

Not all plays are written before they are

Exercises

1.   If you have been lucky enough to have seen a play, can you tell the class about it?

2. If you had to produce Derek Walcott's *Pantomime* outdoors, where would you stage it? What would be the problems you would have to overcome, and how would you overcome them? What would be the benefits of staging it outdoors?

3. What other writers you have ever heard of who are famous for their plays and poetry? What about poetry and songs? Or singing and playing a musical instrument? Are there any other artists you know who can do two artistic things very well?

4. What was your favourite 'play-play' story? Perhaps you still create your own skits? Can you tell your class about them? Children's games are sometimes used by choreographers or singers; have you ever seen or heard any?

6 Dance as theatre

With so many roots traditions having dance and music as integral parts, it is not surprising that the Caribbean has many dance groups. In fact, dance in the Caribbean deserves to be covered in a book by itself. Have you ever read a book or seen a film about dance?

Movement is the most natural means of expression by all living things. Which do you think came first in our lives – sound or movement? Can you give examples to illustrate your views?

All religious rituals, and all folk festivals have an abundance of special movements. Those movements are most often accompanied by music and song of some sort. Do you remember seeing any of these celebrations in which dancing plays an important part? What about pocomania and kumina in Jamaica, or bamboo melodians in St Vincent? How about the colourful La Rose festival and the maypole of St Lucia? Don't forget cumfa, kalimai puja, mari-mari and queh-queh of Guyana, and **tuk-band**, land-ship and service-o'-song in Barbados. Other places have tea-meetings, goombay, jonkanoo and hossein. Some of those names may mean nothing to you, but wouldn't it be an exciting education for you to get to know about them?

Is not a discotheque a sort of ritual, with its music, movements and dancing? It even has a special language and its own behaviour patterns. Add the disco lighting, the effects of repetitive rythms and you have some of the ingredients of certain religious ceremonies with all their theatrical effects. Add the human relationships growing up around the disco (boy meets girl, romance and jealousy and friendships), and you then have drama.

The music and drama in all of these traditions have inspired dance and drama groups to adapt them for use on stage. While writers of plays are called playwrights, those who create dances and arrange and invent the dance steps and patterns are called choreographers.

In the Caribbean, our choreographers have all been influenced by many aspects of the region's cultures. The recent history of stage dancing is very much like that of drama. Before 1945, the only stage dancing your parents might have seen or taken part in would most likely have been English square-dancing, or European ballet and ballroom dance.

What kind of dances have you seen performed on stage during the last year? Did any of them tell a story of any kind? Did that story tell of life in the Caribbean?

Dance is a very expressive art, and can be a most powerful means of telling stories. European ballets are entire full-length plays told in dance and music. The Japanese and East Indians tell intricate and highly dramatic stories with their dance dramas. Every nation has traditional dances which mean important things to them. All African cultures have dances which express various aspects of their lives – the celebration of rain, birth of leaders, praise to their gods, retelling of historic battles, marriage. Caribbean people dance to reggae, calypso and to kumina and hossein with movements that are peculiar to us.

Caribbean stage dancing has been influenced by all the cultures which are part of our history; however, like drama, it took some very special people to emphasize our uniqueness, and to help us use the natural traditions we all have as part of our characters.

The mother of dance in the Caribbean is certainly **Beryl McBurnie** of Trinidad and Tobago. She has done more than any other person to take dance styles away from purely

Theatre is everywhere. Schoolgirls singing and dancing in a national arts festival. Can you tell what kind of building they are in, and in which country? There are clues in the picture. What can be done to those garden spot and flood-lights to improve their effects?

European traditions. She pioneered the concept and the practice of Caribbeanizing dance movements and its choreography. Since the 1940s, Beryl McBurnie has insisted that there are enough exciting, unique folk dances and traditions in the Caribbean for us to draw on as the basis for our own style. She did for dance what the Pantomime did for drama in Jamaica, Louise Bennett did for poetry, and Errol Hill did for drama throughout the region. She founded the Little Carib Theatre way back in 1948, and the work she did in it has influenced the thinking and the performances of hundreds of Caribbean dancers.

A distinctive and beautiful dance style can be seen in Surinam, Trinidad and Guyana where there are many people of East Indian origin. Their centuries-old dance-dramas usually tell stories of their gods and their leaders and heroes. Indian music is quite distinct from any other. Have you ever heard the stringed sitar with its haunting sound, or the twin drums of tablas, or seen kathak dancing with

ankle bells and slapping feet beat out very complex rhythms? In those three countries of the Caribbean, there are cinemas that show nothing else but films made in India; and most Asian-Caribbean people can sing tunes from these highly dramatic stories, which always include many songs and dances, and are usually full of love and adventure.

In all the other islands and countries, there are not so many people of East Indian origin, so that the predominant roots would be European and African. It is the African background which has been deliberately emphasized over the past 30 years.

Just as Jamaican drama is varied and of a high quality, so is its dance. Their best known choreographer/dancer is **Rex Nettleford**. He learned ballet while a student at Oxford University in England, then studied American **modern dance**, absorbed the African traditions, and researched Jamaican folk rituals. In 1963, along with Eddie Thomas, another talented dancer/choreographer, Nettleford founded Jamaica's National Dance Company.

In just over 20 years of existence, that company has become a dominant force in the development of dance theatre in Jamaica, and indeed in the rest of the Caribbean. Its influence helped lead to the founding of a National School of Dance in 1970. Most of all, the company has helped audiences discover Jamaica's heritage, through its many exciting and dramatic dances. The National Dance company draws from many sources – Jamaican, Caribbean, African, Afro-American, modern, European classical ballet, jazz.

Every dance expresses some human feeling, and sometimes a distinct story. Is that not also good drama? After all, steps are the words, language and dialogue of dance. Nettleford's *Pocomania* has been acclaimed by many people as one of his most exciting choreographies, and it takes its steps, style and rhythms from the rituals and ceremonies of the Pocomania religion which is peculiar to Jamaica.

Rex Nettleford agrees that he was greatly influenced by the work of Beryl McBurnie and her devotion to the folk dances of the Caribbean. In dance, as in drama, one person influences the work of another's, and helps to alter and shape his or her growth. That is why it is so important for more exchanges of theatre practitioners to continue throughout the region. Chapter 9 on *Sharing* explains more about the exchange of experiences among the Caribbean's dramatists.

A play is usually written before it is produced, and all good plays have a script of some sort at least after the performance; but the choreography of a dance is not as easily recorded although there are certain written ways of doing this. After a dance number is performed in the Caribbean however, the choreography is normally only in the memory of the dancers and the choreographer. This makes it difficult for dances created in one island to be done by a dance company in another island. The use of videotape could be of great importance to the development of dance. Unfortunately there is very little use of these modern technical facilities among modern theatre practitioners. Why do you think this is so? And what are some of the ways dancers could use these recordings to help with the

growth of Caribbean dance? Does your school use video or even colour-slides to illustrate any of its subjects?

Like drama in the Caribbean, there have been many outstanding dances created by exceptional choreographers who got their inspirations from the everyday life and traditional cultures of the people of the region.

Gora Singh of Guyana presented at Carifesta '72 in Guyana, a moving solo dance of the Lord's Prayer as an example of a mixture of cultures and styles. To the recorded singing of Italian opera singer Mario Lanza, Gora dressed in Indian costume, and mimed/danced the words, using a combination of European and East Indian gestures.

In 1976, two young St Lucian dancers, a Catholic priest and a poet devised and choreographed a one-hour dance drama of the Easter story of Christ's betrayal, trial, crucifixion and rising. They were Michael Francis and Carlton Ishmael with Father Patrick Anthony and Robert Lee. *Moments* was narrated in patois and standard English, with a choir and musicians, and with all the action in dance and mime. They used any style which was

Dance as an expressive means of telling a story is the belief of the Caribbean Dance Theatre in St Croix. This is *Broo Nanci win Snake*. What other animals are there?

appropriate – African, ballet, modern and Caribbean. It was a striking production, but unfortunately never to be seen outside of St Lucia.

However, the Theatre Dance Company of St Croix has made a 16 mm colour-film of a 30-minute ballet, *Buddhoe*. It was choreographed by one-time European ballerina Atti Bermudez, and tells the story of a slave hero of that island who helped to gain freedom from slavery in the 19th century, from the Danes who owned the island at the time. Although at least eight islands have television, the film has not been broadcast outside of St Croix. So the problem of sharing continues.

Trinidadian schoolteacher Astor Johnson, who is one of the outstanding choreographers in the Caribbean, has created a dance he named *Graveyard for the Living*. He used African, American modern, and mime with a specially composed song by one of Trinidad's most talented musicians, **Andrè Tanker**. The story is of a man who is put in a Trinidad jail, and is so shocked by the ill-treatment that he gets, that he commits suicide. As with many deaths, it is the living who suffer the death the most – his mother is broken-hearted for the rest of her life. It is a sad and very moving dance/drama.

At the open-air stage in the museum in Barbados, there is a twice weekly show called *1627 and All That*. It uses traditional dance to tell some of the history of the island. One of its choreographers is Cynthia Wilson of the Barbados Dance Theatre. She includes old-time stick-licking (stick fighting), tuk-band music and dance, the stilt-man, a fishing village scene, a plantation owner's ballroom party,

and childrens' games. The audiences, who are mainly tourists from North America and Europe, are able to get a flavour of the island's background, and a hint of its varied cultural traditions – all within ninety minutes of effective theatre.

Monty Thompson and Jill Wilson, founders and directors of the Caribbean Dance Company in St Croix, formed the group to present Caribbean cultures and tradition in dance form. They research their themes with great care before choreographing and presenting their shows. They both believe in the power of dance as the most expressive means of telling their stories. The Caribbean Dance Company supports five of the group as fulltime professionals, while all the other members are paid small fees for any production dancing or work they may do and are, therefore, semi-professionals.

Exercises

1. How can dance tell a story? What particular dance movements would describe how people feel, what they are doing, and what they are saying to each other? Can you show any of those you have seen?

2. What are the theatrical things which stage-dance performances need to make them interesting and dramatic? Describe some of those techniques you have seen.

3. What special qualities do good dancers need? What sort of training do they take? Have you ever seen a dance class? Describe it if you can.

4. There are many more female dancers than there are male. Why do you think that is so?

7 Musical theatre

As we have seen in previous chapters, theatre is all around us in the Caribbean. The natural dialects of every-day conversation can be a more dramatic way of telling some stories than the standard English we are taught in schools. Many of us have seen or taken part in some sort of carnival celebration, heard a tamboo-bamboo or tuk-band, been to a calypso tent, or stopped to listen to a street-corner preacher. But how many of us have seen a Caribbean musical play in an actual theatre, with a mixture of all the colourful speech, music, song and dance that are of our daily lives, presented right up there on stage?

On many islands during the 1930s and 1940s, the English people living there formed drama groups and operatic societies to present the kind of theatre they knew and loved from their own country. They produced straight plays by Noel Coward and Shakespeare, then operettas by Gilbert and Sullivan, and later began to stage Broadway musicals such as *Guys and Dolls*, *Fiddler on the Roof*, or *West Side Story*. Have you ever heard of any of these? They are all first-class theatre, using the backgrounds, traditions, languages and cultures of the people who made them, and for the audiences who saw them. But they were not in any way from the Caribbean.

These companies staged the theatre that was familiar to them, and their audiences were generally their friends, and Caribbean people who had been exposed to, and appreciated these good North American plays. These lavish productions provided a training ground for many young, native-born talents who are shaping the direction of Caribbean theatre today.

These talented men and women took note of the vast gap between the operettas and musicals they were presenting on stage, and the kind of theatre they knew from their living experiences. As they slicked back their hair and slipped into dinner jackets to sing **Cole Porter** tunes on stage, they began to think of ways to bring the calypso rhythms, colourful dialects and energetic dances that they experienced on the streets and in backyards, into the formal theatre. And slowly we began to see some changes.

Pantomime

The musical theatre with the longest continuous tradition in the Caribbean today is the Jamaican annual Pantomime. It was first staged in 1941 at Kingston's Ward Theatre. The Pantomime is a good example of how, over the years, a European theatrical tradition has been changed to reflect life in the Caribbean.

The Little Theatre Movement (LTM), which produces the annual Pantomime, began as a committee to raise funds for the construction of a theatre of its own. The group decided to raise the money by staging a musical play. That first pantomime, *Jack and the Beanstalk*, and all the early pantomime musicals were strictly within the European tradition. They were fairy tales or fantasies, staged during the Christmas season; the young male romantic lead character was always played by a girl, and the comic 'dame' was a man.

The show's ambition was to be English, and at first it was very typically so. As early as 1943, this began to change, when Elinor Lithgow directed *Soliday and the Wicked Bird*, which was adapted from a Jamaican Anancy story.

The English husband and wife team of Henry and Greta Fowler, originators and producers of the Pantomime in its early years, made a con-

In the Dorsch Center open-air theatre, Fredericksted, St Croix, actors and audience are within touching distance. Is it strange, too, to see actors with their backs to their audience? The American musical play, *Fiddler on the Roof*, was one of the most popular productions of the Courtyard Players.

scious attempt to reflect Jamaican life in each successive show. The choice was partly economic; they needed to raise money and wanted to draw the largest possible audience, rather than just to put on a play for a small élite group. But in choice of scripts, dialogue, music, dance, setting, selection of cast, Jamaicans were having more and more influence.

The Pantomime in Jamaica became centred around the Anancy stories, and because all Jamaicans identified with these folktales, it became a popular success. The annual show now runs for about three months to packed houses. The Pantomime has now become an original and fully Jamaican musical play, with local themes, songs, stories, characters, dances, music, scenery, costumes, dialogue and situations. Most of Jamaica's best known actors have performed or worked within this 'modern' theatre tradition, such as Louise Bennett who acted in more than twenty productions.

Jamaica is not alone in staging a Christmas season pantomime. Beginning in 1966, the Barbados Festival Choir has produced a series of original musical plays called *Bimshire* which have been patterned after the Jamaican pantomime. The originators of *Bimshire* were Noel Vaz of the University of the West Indies' Mona campus in Jamaica, and Daphne Hackett, a Barbadian schoolteacher.

Like the Jamaican pantomime, *Bimshire* drew on local music, song and dialogue to tell a fantasy story set in Barbados. One early production, *Loss Ball, Six Runs*, used the Caribbean's most popular sport of cricket as the central story and theme with main character based on the great Sir Gary Sobers. Unfortunately, musical productions require an enormous amount of work and considerable money to stage; and the technical requirements are usually beyond the average drama group's capacity.

We have seen how the annual Christmas Pantomime in Jamaica has become a local

37

tradition as people born and raised on the island brought their own skills, roots, and experiences into shaping this unique musical production.

In looking at production on other islands, we often find that the dedication and talent of a single individual has shaped the musical theatre on a particular island. Here are island-born producer/playwrights who got their first theatre training in classical European theatre. They took that training and their own roots to produce some of the most unique plays in the short history of the musical theatre in the Caribbean. Three such individuals are Alwin Bully of Dominica, Derek Walcott of St Lucia, and Henk Tjon of Suriname.

Alwin Bully

Alwin is founder and leader of the Peoples' Action Theatre group in Dominica which has produced all of his plays, among which were two colourful and popular musicals, **Pio Pio** and *Folk Nativity*. The first is a patriotic musical play which he created specially for a national celebration. *Folk Nativity* is his Christmas play, but it is relocated in a mixture of Caribbean and African settings.

Bully designed the costumes, scenery, lighting, wrote the script and lyrics, and helped to compose the music. He has been influenced in his designs, and some of the music by his island's Carnival celebrations. The cadence rhythm, which originated in the French islands of Martinique and Guadeloupe, is also a feature of his work. Other aspects of Alwin Bully's work in theatre are described in Chapter 5 called *Plays, Players and Playwrights*.

Derek Walcott

There must be very few theatre artists whose work is more varied than Derek Walcott's, born in St Lucia, but who has been living in Trinidad for the past 25 years. His musical plays have been produced in many Caribbean territories. Like his straight plays, Walcott's musicals differ in style but share a similar theme – the various confusions which Caribbean people feel because of our 400-year history of slavery, colonialism, and very recent independence for most countries. He has written and directed five musical plays. Among them are *Ti-Jean and His Brothers*, and **The Joker of Seville**, both of which were very popular in Trinidad and Tobago. They have both been performed in other Caribbean territories, and also in America and Canada.

Ti-Jean and His Brothers is about a poor woman living in the mountainous St Lucian rain-forests with her three sons. The Devil makes an agreement with her: if any one of the sons can defeat him, that son could have any wish fulfilled. The two older brothers lose, and

Stage costumes influenced by Carnival in Dominica. *Pio Pio* had twenty new songs which Alwin Bully helped to compose in five days!

38

Song and dance, design, costumes and scenic art are all parts of Alwin Bully's *Folk Nativity*. This musical toured several islands to raise funds for stricken Dominica immediately after Hurricane David in 1979. This is an example of theatre used for national development.

the Devil eats them. The youngest son, Ti-Jean (*petit* John, or little John) beats the Devil by disobeying and tricking him in the true Anancy tradition. He burns down the Devil's cane-fields instead of counting all the leaves as he was told to do; he also is able to defeat the magic of the Devil's goat, which no one can tether, by castrating it.

This musical play is a Caribbean fairy tale containing all the usual ingredients of magic, good versus evil, talking birds and animals, folk songs, patois, and a happy ending. It also uses religious music, and specially composed songs including some in calypso style. It is an ideal play for schools.

On the other hand, The *Joker of Seville* is a more complex adult play, with the use of both Standard English and Trinidad first language in dialogue and songs. It was created by Derek Walcott when the Royal Shakespeare Company in England asked him to adapt a seventeenth century Spanish play. That play was *El Burlador de Sevilla* by the playwright Tirso de Molina. The leading character is Don Juan, a handsome Spaniard who is loved by all the women he meets, both in Spain and the Caribbean. The music is a mixture of romantic Spanish tunes and Caribbean calypso. Walcott gave his play a strong Caribbean flavour, for example, by adapting a swordfencing scene into a stick-fight, complete with kalinda drumming and speechifying:

> You better watch yourself old man,
> Nobody can beat Don Juan.
> Send one man or ten thousand,
> Nobody can beat Don Juan.

Henk Tjon

So far, the musicals described were written and produced for the usual proscenium stages, and follow the usual style of most plays. Henk Tjon, director of the Doe (pronounced doo) Theatre in Surinam often breaks these traditional ways of producing plays in the Caribbean.

Although Surinam is not an English-speaking Caribbean territory, almost everybody speaks English, and it shares historic and cultural ties with the rest of the Caribbean, and Henk Tjon is very active in the development of Caribbean theatre.

The productions of Henk Tjon mix many styles and traditions. He sometimes uses very few actors, but sometimes he stages a very large and lavish presentation. In many of his works, five actors on stage have to play several parts, and all of them have to mime, dance, sing and act. The music is specially composed with a mixture of styles. Sometimes he uses folktales, and often he refers to political situations.

In the seven-person play *Stages*, Tjon and his co-playwright Thea Doelwijte present a history of slavery, colonialism, modern-day independence and political corruption, all within a single production. The seven actors all had to

Ti-Jean meets the Devil at an open-air production in the Christiansted Fort in St Croix. What are the pros and cons of open-air theatre like this?

dance, talk, sing and switch their roles in an instant. The dialogue spoken in one scene was invented by the actors, but sounded like some unknown ancient language, and still had to sound as if it was understood by all; it also had to give the exact feeling of intended emotions and meanings to the audience. Naturally the script of this play, if there is any, would be difficult to make – particularly as the production was rehearsed using the improvization technique; and it is very likely that if it is done again by another group, the exact words and actions would not be repeated.

His *Rebirth*, staged at the Carifesta '81 in Barbados used characters, dances, music and songs from the different cultures and races which make up his socially mixed country. It was a lavish and fully costumed play designed to show-off the many and exciting cultures and traditions of Surinam, and also to give a message of the need for racial and cultural harmony among people.

Roderick Walcott

Yet another playwright who has used folk traditions to create musical plays is Roderick Walcott, the twin brother of Derek. He has written three plays which use the St Lucian street theatre of the La Rose Festival as the central setting and theme. One of them, **Banjo Man** was seen at the first Carifesta in Guyana in 1972. Its main character was Estophan, the banjo-man of the Festival, and the play includes a dramatic presentation of the rituals of that unique St Lucian tradition. If you are fortunate to have a St Lucian classmate, you may be able to persuade her or him to tell you about La Rose.

Helen Camps

So far, we have looked at some of the ways in which innovative Caribbean people have brought our cultural traditions onto stages, in

40

Every actor in Tjon's theatre has to sing, dance, act, mime and be physically fit to keep up the continuous action. Henk Tjon is seated on the right, and that is Pandora Gibson-Gomez standing centre. The actors from six different Caribbean countries shared their skills in this production of *Stages*.

the form of musical plays of various styles. Now let us look at another creative producer and writer. Helen Camps of Trinidad and Tobago uses musical theatre to help preserve some of the disappearing cultural traditions, particularly those associated with carnival.

Unlike Bully, Walcott or Tjon, Helen Camps was not Caribbean-born. She came to Trinidad from Ireland in the 1960s, and brought with her a European theatre background.

Over the years, she watched the oldest traditional characters of carnival being pushed out of the way by the huge masked bands which now fill the streets in a colourful procession each year. She worried about what would happen to the Midnight Robber and to Pierrot Grenade with their clever speechifying. What would come of the dancing of **Jab Molassi**, the Minstrels and to the animal-and-rider Borokit?

For Helen Camps, the answer was to bring these old-time characters onto the formal stage, along with calypsonians and the steelband, in a new style of musical theatre which she calls *Carnival Theatre*. There have always been some sort of dramatic presentations within the Carnival celebrations, including the still popular Ol'Mas night of humorous and satirical skits, but this was the first full-length stage

play which attempted so thoroughly to integrate all the traditions.

In 1980, she produced the first-ever full-length stage play in which all the characters were taken straight out of traditional carnival. The main characters in *Mas in Yuh Mas* were the threatening Midnight Robber, and picong-expert Pierrot Grenade. The musical accompaniment included a fully costumed Minstrel band, which played many old-time calypsoes, and some new songs specially written for the play by a young composer named Roger Israel.

Helen Camps followed this with two more Carnival plays – *King Jab Jab* and *Jouvert*. She also directed and produced three new costumed, Christmas musicals, *Cinderama*, *Snokone and the Seven Dwens* and *Ad*. In all of her work, she is directly influenced by the colours and gaiety of Carnival, varied folk traditions, and by rock and other popular music. Perhaps she has started a new musical tradition. During 1982 she toured England and Europe with *Jouvert*, and opened the Tent Theatre in Port-of-Spain.

It is interesting to note that Paul Keens-Douglas used her Tent Theatre once a week during the 1983 Carnival season, for his first-ever *Talk Tent*. In this, he produced shows in which only comedians, dialect poets, extempo and **picong** artists performed. Here, suddenly, are two new kinds of Caribbean formal theatre going on at the same time, and both assisting each other. Paul wrote *Mas in Yuh Mas* and acted in it, and Helen's canvas tent, pitched in Port-of-Spain, housed both her Carnival Theatre and his Talk Tent.

It is relevant to note here, that the lavish all-day competition of the parade of mas' bands across the 300 foot stage at Trinidad's carnival has been seeing some very striking changes. A theatre designer, Peter Minshall, has been introducing theatrical designs in his costumes. In 1978, he brought on 1500 players with huge animal skulls and brown macramé skirts, which he called *Dance Macabre*. Then in 1983 he put 2500 players in all white costumes, then had them come on the huge stage, before 15,000 people, and drench themselves in bright coloured dyes. In both cases, he was

King Jab Jab and his court. That small stool in the bottom of this picture was the only stage 'scenery' in the production *Mas in Yuh Mas*. If there is no scenery, what are the other things needed to keep the audience interested, and to know where the action is taking place?

emphasising the evil and ugliness which lay beneath the surface of the bright tinsel of society; and in both cases, the judges placed his band far down the line, because they thought his designs and themes were too harsh for the traditional *pretty mas* of carnival. Minshall's participation has caused much controversy in Trinidad about the effect of introducing such theatrical social comment into this area which otherwise involves colourful and happy costume bands.

There is little doubt that the colourful, dramatic traditions of the Caribbean can continue to be a fruitful source of musical theatre for years to come. Perhaps the greatest restraint on this type of theatre has been the cost in time and money of organization and production but it also true that it is very difficult to gather together the quantity and variety of artists necessary to produce a musical play. However, in the last few years, more and more drama groups and directors have acquired the skills, techniques, finances and confidence to undertake the enormous amount of work required for such productions. Can we therefore, expect to see a continued interest and growth in the musical theatre of the Caribbean?

Exercises

1. You may be surprised to discover how many songs you probably know, or at least hear, on the radio, which have come from musical plays. Can you identify just one of them and the play it came from? Imagine the situation in which the song was sung.

2. Choose any three songs you know and create a story around them. Or choose any Anancy story you know and put three songs into the story at appropriate points. The songs can be of any style – pop, kaiso, folk, childrens', funk, soul.

3. Do you know of any local musicals? Ask your parents if they have seen any, and, if they have, to teach you one of the songs, and tell you the story of the play. Tell the class what you have learned.

4. Have you seen any folk festivals or rituals such as masquerades, jonkanoo, La Rose or hossein? Write a short story with any of these as the central theme. It may be about one of the participants, or about your own experiences during a festival, or just a description of it.

5. Take any poem you know and perform it to any suitable kind of tune or rhythm.

6. Why do you think you have not heard any of the songs in the Caribbean musicals mentioned in this chapter? What needs to be done so that some of them become popular in the region?

8 Other forms

There are many other types of theatre which are part of the total Caribbean scene. Many hardworking artists and organizers have produced a variety of theatrical forms, which all add to the enrichment of the cultural and artistic life of the Caribbean. You must have seen or perhaps even been involved in at least two of the following kinds of theatre available in the region.

Nightclubs

Many people like to be entertained by some form of theatre when they go out in the evening to a nightclub. They may dine, have a few drinks with friends, and then 'take in a show'. Many big hotel restaurants have basic facilities for shows, either in the restaurant itself or in an adjoining room. Night club shows usually contain a series of variety acts: master of ceremonies, singer, limbo dancer, fire-eater, calypsonian, a group of folksingers or dancers, and a small orchestra. These acts are popular with most tourists who come from North America or Europe.

The limbo is a particularly exciting type of theatre; an horizontal bar hangs less than a foot from the floor with a dancer inching her or his way under it. Some daring performers use flaming crossbars. There are several theories about the origin of this particular dance. What do you think is its origin?

Dinner theatre

A very few enterprising restaurants offer dinner guests a straight play as after-dinner entertainment. This is not widespread in the Caribbean, but deserves some consideration as a possible development.

One of the most complete dinner theatres was presented at the Normandie Hotel in Trinidad between 1979 and 1982. After dinner, a full-length play was presented on a stage which covered nearly one-third of the dining-room. The plays were usually comedies, as it was felt that diners would not want 'heavy' theatre as an after-dinner entertainment. This series was started by Trevor Rhone, but was taken over in 1980 by actress/director Judy Stone, who ran six plays a year. During the four years it was in operation, the Normandie Dinner Theatre paid all of its performers and technicians, and provided acting opportunities to dozens of Trinidadians in the twenty plays it produced. This dinner theatre closed in 1982, but Judy Stone continues to produce new plays in Port-of-Spain.

During 1983, there were two dinner theatres in St Croix and St Thomas (US Virgin Islands). They produced good American comedies, but their commercial successes were not always assured.

A producer in Barbados broke the tradition for this nightclub type of entertainment by presenting a musical comedy based on a famous historical woman of Barbados, Rachel Pringle. It was named **Barbados Barbados.** During the interval a buffet dinner was served. It ran every Tuesday evening for two years in an old boiler-room which was converted specially for the production. It became very popular with visiting tourists, for whom it was written by Ken Corsbie and an English woman, Julia Senior.

Dinner theatre is an established and successful form of presentation in North America, but is still to be fully explored as an artistic and commercially profitable enterprise in the Caribbean. The next time your school pro-

1. Supper is over, diners are feeling good, after-dinner drinks are on the tables, everybody shifts their chairs to enjoy the dinner theatre play.
2. On a fully designed stage, Judy Stone and Nigel Scott in the American play *Dry Run*. The low ceiling (less than 8 feet) was both an asset and a liability. Why?

duces a play or variety show, you may wish to consider having one night as a dinner theatre, and promote it among your parents and their friends.

Radio and television

These two broadcasting media have a great influence on the everyday life of Caribbean people. Every territory has at least one radio station. Yet, except for one or two outstanding exceptions, these stations do not encourage or produce any regular drama of a Caribbean nature. All the series and serials and plays you see on television are imported from the big distributing agencies in North America and England.

The stations do not all have personnel who can direct plays for radio or television, and most stage directors and actors do not have experience in producing for these media. Television drama costs much more to produce locally than to rent from abroad; and it also needs special skills and expensive technical facilities.

Among the very few small private television production companies which produce valuable cultural and artistic programmes is the Banyan Studio in Trinidad. They have pro-

duced three short drama serials and many documentaries of the performing arts. They shot Carifesta '81 in Barbados and made an exciting programme out of this important festival. The key persons in Banyan are Chris Laird and Bruce Paddington.

Trinidad and Tobago's television stations tried to produce a Caribbean play each month for several years. Although the budget allocated to this exercise was impractically low, the director of drama, Horace James, somehow managed to mount a production most of the time. Jamaica has television and radio stations with their own drama departments, and these have produced long-running serials for radio, and some good television drama. Guyana Broadcasting Service has been very helpful to local playwrights by producing many of their radio plays and serials. Have you ever seen or heard any of these? Does it appear odd that these stations do not make arrangements to have these programmes exchanged?

Producing radio plays is much cheaper than it is for the stage, and presents fewer problems. All it really needs is a good tape-recorder, a couple of microphones, a quiet room, and some imagination and practice. You may even be able to obtain some assistance from your local radio station, particularly if you are in one of the smaller islands.

Cinema

Making a full-length feature film is an expensive and technically complex undertaking. It requires an enormous number of highly skilled people. There have been many films made in the Caribbean by American producers, but relatively few by Caribbean writers, directors, actors and companies.

However, the naturally beautiful scenery, interesting variety of people, music and cultures have inspired the making of some interesting films. Have you ever heard of *The Harder They Come*, in which a reggae singer in Jamaica finds himself forced into crime? It was a breakthrough in Caribbean films, and has become an international favourite. Trevor Rhone's *Smile Orange* was also popular throughout the Caribbean; and Trinidad produced a sensitively written and directed film,

Bim, which tells the story of an Indian-Trinidadian country boy who comes to town, where he fights racial and class discrimination. He eventually becomes a powerful political figure, but still finds himself a victim of the system.

Bim was banned in Guyana because of its 'racial overtones', suspended in Trinidad because of 'obscene language', and censored in Jamaica because of its 'gun violence'. Race and class prejudice, political comment, and the use of language are serious issues to be tackled in the arts. This issue deserves serious discussion, and must be faced honestly and bravely if we are to break out of narrow constraints on concepts and ideas. In the Caribbean, there is always a continuous concern about censorship in many spheres of our lives, and you should be aware of these concerns if you are going to get into any artistic fields, particularly drama. Why do you think that drama is the most censored of the arts?

One of the few plays produced in 15 years by the Barbados television station was *The Tout* by Errol John of Trinidad. Have you ever been in a TV station? What would you expect to find there, and what would be the differences as compared with the stage of a theatre?

45

An example of the one-ness of the Caribbean, and the need for interaction among artists from various countries in order to grow together. *Ti-Jean and his Brothers*, as produced by Stage One, was shot in Barbados by a Trinidadian and Guyanese crew, directed by a Guyanese, with actors from Barbados, Guyana and Trinidad. The playwright is St Lucian. Most of this play was shot in Welchman's Hall Gully, the only rain-forest in Barbados, by a Banyan technical crew under the direction of Michael Gilkes who produced a one-hour version of the play.

National arts festivals

One very productive national effort which must be commended, not least because of the enormous amount of participation by schools in most of them, is the National Arts Festival which many of the Caribbean countries try to have on a regular basis.

Barbados has its *National Festival of Creative Arts* (NIFCA) in the September term, during which, there is islandwide participation on both the adult and school levels in arts and crafts of a wide variety. Jamaica's annual Festival has been influential in the raising of the amount and quality of the arts, including dance and drama throughout the island. The Jamaican government has created a special Festival Office, which ensures that the organization is efficiently run for the thousands of competitors and the hundreds of shows and exhibitions all over the island.

Trinidad teachers run an annual Secondary Schools Drama Festival, which continues to build up young audiences and performers.

However, the teachers admit that there needs to be a full-time office for this festival, to make sure that there is continuity and growth. They also agree that there needs to be theatre arts in the curriculum of each and every school on the island. Why is this not so by now? What do you think are the factors which hold up this progressive step?

Other countries in the Caribbean have similar festivals which are having positive effects on the development of theatre. GUYFESTA in Guyana is so complex to organize, that the Department of Culture only runs it every two years. You must remember that Guyana is 500 miles by 200 miles, and consists of vast areas of tropical rain-forest, almost unpopulated savannah country, and massive mountain ranges. Neighbouring villages could be 50 miles apart in some places, and therefore the organization of a national arts festival has some special problems. Participation by all schools is still somehow achieved, and some very exciting work comes out of these children.

In 1983, the Island Centre Theatre in St Croix

organized its first-ever national schools drama festival. Across the Caribbean sea, on the Central American coast, Belize used to have a national arts festival, but lack of full governmental and other support make it impossible to continue regular annual events.

If your country does not have some sort of regular festival in which schools take part in the arts, particularly the performing arts, then only you can ask for some sort of similar activity. Theatre people in all the islands are usually willing to assist in such a project; and teachers will be your best allies to help you in arousing interest, and to give the support which you will need. Start small — perhaps an inter-house or inter-class festival — then move on to inter-school between two friendly schools. You would have to consider carefully whether you would want to stress the competitiveness or the involvement; some people feel that the arts should not be too competitive, but a sharing and a joy.

Exercises

1. Your school has decided to start dinner theatre in its assembly hall, or dining room, canteen or gymnasium. What are the things to consider to get it done efficiently? Design a useful stage with its lighting and other necessary facilities, without being too elaborate. Choose four plays for the season.

2. Is there one type of entertainment for tourists, and another for local audiences? Can there be a type of theatre which would interest both audiences?

3. What would be the differences in writing, directing and acting for stage, radio, television and feature films? Take a short scene from a play you may be doing for your CXC exam, or for an end-of-term entertainment, and act it out in four different ways — for the stage, radio, television and the feature film. This will help to make the differences clearer.

9 Sharing

It could be argued that one of the main factors which slows down development of drama in the region is the lack of any regular inter-island exchange between theatre groups and individuals. There is very little touring of productions between islands. The radio and television stations do not produce or broadcast many plays, and the few that they do produce are not heard or seen by audiences outside that particular country. Apart from the excellent series of plays published by the UWI's Extra Mural department in Trinidad in the 1960s, there have been very few play scripts published over the last 20 years. Carifesta comes irregularly, and no one country is likely to experience it more than once in 20 years.

The reasons for this isolation are many. After examining and discussing this question, can you think of some reasons for it?

One of the accepted ways for progress to occur is through regular exchange and sharing of ideas and skills. A school is a formal way of exchanging ideas. CARICOM was set up to unite, develop and exchange economic efforts in all the Caribbean territories. The Caribbean Development Bank is a shared financial resource. The UWI offers a shared tertiary education. The CXC was set up so that you could share a common, relevant syllabus. Perhaps the best example of sharing is the West Indies Cricket team which has been one of the best in the world for many years now.

Carifesta

We are fortunate in the Caribbean to have a festival in which all the arts can be experienced over a fortnight of hectic activity. In 1972, the Guyanese government organized the first Caribbean Festival of the Arts. All countries bordering the Caribbean sea were invited to participate. There were art exhibitions, seminars, musical concerts, plays, dance recitals, folk choirs and traditional street performances.

Artists of all types and nationalities had their first opportunity to see each other's works and to meet with each other. Dramatists had the chance to see new plays and styles. They saw and met with best actors in the region, doing well-directed productions of groups from everywhere. It was a unique and exhilarating experience for all concerned. Have you been lucky enough to have attended performances at any of the four Carifestas? What did you learn from the shows?

Among the many excellent plays they saw during the four festivals up to 1983 were:

— **Couvade** in Guyana. A play about the racial mixtures in the region.
— **Mother Poem**. A dramatization of a series of poems by Barbadian Edward Brathwaite. It used colour-slides, film, actors and dancers, and taped music and voices.
— **In the Castle of My Skin**. A specially re-written version of a novel by George Lamming of Barbados.
— **The Dragon Can't Dance**. A staged reading of a novel by Trinidadian Earl Lovelace.
— **Dog** by Dennis Scott of Jamaica. A powerful play about social revolution. Half of the cast play dogs rebelling against their masters.

There have been other Carifestas in Jamaica (1976), Cuba (1979) and Barbados (1981), but they have all been costly, and extremely difficult to organize to everybody's satisfaction.

Striking design, costumes and make-up are all essential parts of *Couvade*, produced by the Jamaica School of Drama, which also included music, songs, chants, Amerindian rituals, a street preacher. The playwright, Michael Gilkes, included a strong message of the necessity for unity among Caribbean people.

There are a myriad of things to be carefully planned and executed. Can you think of some of these? Remember that invitations go to all the countries which border the Caribbean sea, and there could be up to 1500 artists in your country during the two weeks. If your country was hosting Carifesta, can you imagine what problems would have to be overcome?

Unfortunately, two years after the 1981 Carifesta in Barbados, it has not yet been decided where and when the fifth festival would be held. What would be needed to ensure continuity and improvement of Carifestas in the future?

Theatre Information Exchange

Recognizing the need for growth through sharing and inter-action, a few concerned and enterprising theatre practitioners did something about it. In 1976, on the Morne mountain overlooking Castries, the capital of St Lucia, 22 dramatists from 11 English-speaking Caribbean territories met for the first time. They founded the **Theatre Information Exchange**, (TIE). It was a private organization, and the funding for that historic meeting was met by the Inter American Foundation in the USA. The purpose of the new association was to be a central source of information, and a common meeting ground for all those involved in the theatre. Although its main emphasis and interest was in drama (just as this book is), it actively encouraged dancers and musicians to participate, because it recognized that today's Caribbean theatre is a mixture of all the arts, and all the cultural traditions.

In 1978, again with funding from the IAF, Ken Corsbie was appointed as full-time coordinator for two years, and an office was set up in Barbados. During the next three years, theatre practitioners from at least 13 territories became much more aware of each other. With awareness came interest in each other's welfare and development, and with interest came the practical exchange of experiences and skills. They met again in Barbados during 1978, and in 1981 in St Thomas, US Virgin Islands.

Caribuste

While TIE was helping to unite the region's dramatists, another useful organization was formed in Trinidad. The Caribbean United States Theatre Exchange (CARIBUSTE) was created to be a bridge between dramatists in the region and in the USA.

Between 1979 and 1982 there were three meetings of theatre practitioners from the Caribbean and the USA at Caribuste meetings. These meetings climaxed with the first Caribbean Playwrights' Conference in St Thomas. At that historic meeting, six new Caribbean plays were staged to give the writers the opportunity to see their works under critical conditions. Among the lessons learned, was that a play can be read for the first time, cast, rehearsed and staged for an invited audience in only three days! Although the cast all had the scripts in hand during performances, the appreciative audiences gave some of these plays a standing ovation.

Have you ever had playreading sessions with any of the scripts from the CXC syllabus? Would you dare try to do what was done in St Thomas? Take nine days, if you wish, over two weekends. It is very possible and exciting; and you may learn more in this way about the play than from a year of studying it from the book only.

Partly as a result of the efforts of TIE and CARIBUSTE, many exchanges of theatre productions and personnel have taken place; and they continue to occur because of the person-to-person meetings. One of the most important things the dramatists learned from these meetings and communication with each other was that growth can be faster and more fully realized, if they all work together in the development process.

Among the very many examples of sharing and inter-action resulting from TIE and CARIBUSTE were:

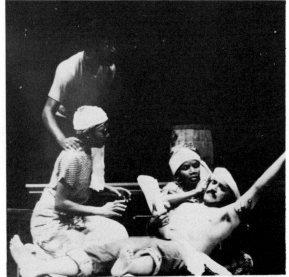

A highly emotional death scene in *Pelee* at the Playwrights' Conference in St Thomas. What is unusual in this scene?

— Two of David Edgecombe's plays have been produced in the Cayman Islands by the Inn Theatre.
— The Jamaica School of Drama ran two workshops in Barbados and one in Grand Cayman.
— The Hippodrome Theatre in Gainesville, Florida, and the Actors' Theatre in Minneapolis, both in the USA, have produced different versions of Walcott's *Pantomime* with Wilbert Holder (Trinidad) as one of the actors.
— Stage One in Barbados has produced the CXC choice, *Moon on a Rainbow Shawl*, Walcott's *Pantomime* and *Ti-Jean and His Brothers*.
— The Eugene O'Neill Theatre in Connecticut has printed and circulated a directory of Caribbean theatre groups and playwrights. (Its director, George White, is also the founder and chairman of CARIBUSTE.)
— Henk Tjon has conducted his unique workshops in Trinidad, Barbados and St Thomas.
— Helen Camp's production of *Mas in Yuh Mas* has toured Grenada.
— Ken Corsbie has performed his one-man show *We-One* in Grand Cayman, St Croix, St Thomas, Guyana and in Gainesville, Florida.
— Errol Jones, the Trinidad actor has starred in and toured with **Kirnon's Kingdom** to several of the islands.
— Francis Lewis the lighting technician has conducted a workshop in Barbados.
— An American playwright/actor, James Cada, was invited to Trinidad by Judy Stone to act in his two-man play *Old Explorers* with Horace James.

Throughout those active years, no Caribbean Government or commercial organization made any substantial financial contribution to TIE or Caribuste. Have you ever heard of either of these organizations? If not, why not?

The latest association of regional theatre personnel and groups was formed in 1983 with the Eastern Caribbean Popular Theatre Organ-

Frank and open discussion about the plays, after each performance, was an important part of the Playwrights' Conference. What would you need to do to ensure these critiques remained constructive and productive? Fifty theatre practitioners from fifteen Caribbean territories and the USA participated in this historic conference.

ization (ECPTO). Its aims include the examination and utilization of popular theatre methods, which can help to effect communities in positive ways. Their first workshop was held in St Vincent, at which there were theatre practitioners from several islands. Its first chairperson was Blazer Williams, who is a popular playwright in St Vincent.

There can be no doubt that theatre in the Caribbean has come a long way; but it still has a long way to go to be truly accepted by education systems, the media, or by the business sections of the community. It also has a long way to go to develop fully its skills among all the practitioners themselves. Like cricket, football, literature, medicine, mathematics, so too, theatre needs to start somewhere in the school systems with its hundreds of thousands of students like yourselves, sharing your experiences. Sharing, after all, is what theatre is all about.

Exercises

1. Note the name of one of David Edgecombe's plays produced by the Inn Theatre? Why do you think the name was altered? How can the creators of other works of art be pressured to change? Do you know of any songs or plays or performances which have been altered or banned?

2. Do you think Governments should assist organizations such as TIE or CARIBUSTE? What are the pros and cons of such assistance?

3. As an ongoing project, would your class undertake the writing of a book on the theatre in your own country? If you dare to do this, it would justify the very hard work being done by every artist in your community. You would have shared your talents, and contributed to the development of theatre in the Caribbean. And you would have enjoyed it, and discovered some interesting facts.

10 Theatre tomorrow

We have looked very briefly at parts of the mosaic which make up the history of Caribbean theatre. But this is only a very small piece of the total story. **Other books** on theatre have been written, and hopefully others are being written and published at this moment, which will present different aspects and viewpoints of this vast area of Caribbean life.

If you have become interested in theatre in the Caribbean, you might spend many years studying it. Perhaps you will actually participate as an actor, director, designer, technician, producer, or as the vitally necessary informed and sympathetic member of our audiences, for the rest of your life.

In order to understand the present theatre in the Caribbean, and to forecast for tomorrow, it is necessary to remember the past, and to remind yourselves of some of the many many pieces of the past which make up our present. Someone described this process as 'a backward look into the future'.

What cultures make up the present Caribbean? How do those cultures influence and shape our everyday living, and therefore our formal theatre? Who are the people who made our theatre what it is today? And what are the myriad things which will continue to influence future artists?

You may not know many of the following names and items, but they are all parts of the whole picture. All of our playwrights draw on one or many of them, or others like them. If you ever write a poem or a play, or a calypso, you may be using some part of the following traditions.

Amerindian

The original Caribbean people had a long cultural history of their own, but Imperialism, colonialism and modern disinterest could wipe this culture out of our future. Except in Guyana, there is very little Amerindian influence in the Caribbean's modern dance, drama or songs. Among many rich legends, places and traditions they gave us are the legend of Kaieteur, the Umana Yana, Couvade, exquisite balata sculpture, pepperpot, and rock-drawings. They also still have the Halleluah religion, the Wai Wai and Makushi tribes, their mari-mari dance, and the Caribbean cowboys, the vaqueros, in the wide savannahs of Guyana. Do you know of any of these images in any Caribbean art, dance, songs, or poetry? In Trinidad, many of the parang players have Amerindian ancestry.

Europeans

The Caribbean is still greatly influenced by the *English* educational and political systems. Except for St Lucia and Dominica, our first languages are all dialects derived mostly from English. For more than a hundred years, English theatre, songs, dances and plays were the main formal stage productions. Shakespeare is still probably the most quoted and known playwright in the Caribbean. Then there is cricket, football and the Beatles.

There has not been any direct *Spanish* influence into the English-speaking Caribbean for more than a century; yet in Trinidad and Jamaica, their nameplaces remain: Maracas, San Fernando, Ocho Rios, Sanjuan, Chaquanos. Their beautiful parang Christmas music and songs with quatro, guitars and tam-

Cricket is drama and dance with joy and sadness. Australian batsman Greg Chappell is bowled for a duck (without scoring), and walks unhappily back to the pavilion as the four West Indian fieldsmen leap up and down with joy.

bourine are still very much alive. Did the calypso originally have spanish rhythms?

St Lucia's and Dominica's patois is a *French* dialect. Out of that patois have come some lovely folksongs; and nameplaces abound: Laventille, Soufriere, Roseau. The Walcott twins were influenced by patois. Carnival was a direct result of French influence in the 18th century. The musical speech accents of Trinidadians, Grenadians, St Lucians and Dominicans have that French influence; and was it that accent which helped to gave us calypso?

The *Dutch* left the 100 mile-long seawall of Guyana's coastline, and names like Vreedenhoop, Den Amstel, and the artist family Broodhagen. Surinam's Henk Tjon must have been influenced by his country's mixture of Dutch, Chinese, Indians, Africans and Javanese.

Asians

Chinese chow mein, laundries, and businessmen are common in many countries, but there is very little visible Chinese influence in the arts. However, who can deny their martial arts popularity throughout the Caribbean? Will those movements have some influence with our dancers? Their strong roots of music, dance, clothes do not seem to appear in any of our theatre. Why do you think this is so?

On the other hand, *East Indian* traditions are very much with us in Hossein, Phagwah, tabla and tassa drums, mosques and temples, the

53

sari, dhoti and roti. Then there are cricketers like Ramadhin, Kallicharan and Kanhai. Do not forget the delicate filigree jewellery, and the incredible Lata Mangeshkar, who sang in hundreds of Indian films, and is adored by Indian-Caribbeans in Guyana, Trinidad and Surinam.

Africans

Shango, pocomania, obeah, drums everywhere, Spree Simon and the steelband, folksongs, Bob Marley, Sparrow, limbo, breadfruit, coo-coo, the moko-jumbie or stilt-man, Jah and cornrow hairstyles have found places in our life.

The purpose of naming these things is to jog your memory, and to fill the air with the sound of the music of their names. All these ingredients and much much more make up our Caribbean cultures and therefore our arts. Paul Keens-Douglas and Louise Bennett, Rex Nettleford, Pandora Gibson-Gomez and Marc Matthews are all a result of various combinations of these ingredients and differences.

Our differences and similarities in varying proportions created *Brown Skin Girl*, *The Joker of Seville*, *Smile Orange*, *The Merrymen* of Barbados, Byron Lee the Jamaican musician, *Tanti at the Oval*, *Mas in Yuh Mas*, *No Woman No Cry* and *All-Ah-We*.

Theatre in the Caribbean continues to change and develop. The fact that you are reading this book, and perhaps have read the two previous publications in the series, is evidence that things are changing in our schools. The future is built upon the past, and the present is merely a stepping stone to tomorrow. You are all part of the things your parents are, and many changes in the next twenty years will be made by you. So what will those changes be?

Will the stage change its shape again? Will Carnival theatre spread its influence? How much political, social and religious pressure will *you* place on the theatre of tomorrow? After soca, what is the next change for calypso? What will *you* do to develop the school auditorium into a more productive theatre space? Will Carifesta have served its purpose and fade away?

Theatre in the Caribbean does not present the answers to these questions. It introduces some background, points to some trends, and poses the questions for you. Your own reactions to the theatre in the Caribbean will help to determine the future. The plays and poems you will write and produce and perform during your schooldays *and beyond* will be part of the answers. If you do participate, then you will open yourselves to a lot of very hard work, excitement and learning.

Glossary

This glossary provides further information on the items which appear in bold print in the book. It gives the sources of some of the material, and offers references which may be useful to teachers and students, when they wish to obtain further relevant material, or to make contact with some of the theatre practitioners. Like the photographs and their captions, the glossary supports the written material, and should be seen as integral to better understanding of *Theatre in the Caribbean*.

Page **iii**. *Music in the Caribbean* by John Sealey and Krister Malm, was published in January 1982, and is the first in this series being put out by Hodder and Stoughton. The second book was *Tourism in the Caribbean* by Neil Sealey, published January 1983. Both of these books, like *Theatre in the Caribbean*, are designed as introductions to different aspects of Caribbean life. They may be considered as interdependent, as they often offer different viewpoints of the same subjects.

page **1**. *Cricket Lovely Cricket* by Lord Kitchener was a calypso celebrating the victories of the West Indies Cricket team in England during the 1951 tour. It particularly referred to the bowling of 'spin-twins' Ramadhin (Trinidad) and Valentine (Jamaica), who mesmerized the English batsmen throughout the series.

page **1**. *Moon on a Rainbow Shawl* was published by Faber and Faber, 1971. See Chapter 5 on *Plays, Players and Playwrights* for further information.

page **1**. The Caribbean Examination Council (CXC), with its headquarters in Barbados, was formed by the Caribbean governments, with the intention of altering the subjects, themes and methods being used in the secondary school systems. This was done to make them more relevant to the needs of the region's children, and therefore its future leaders. The high-school graduation examinations are now, for the most part, our own CXC.

page **1**. Michael Gilkes, lecturer of English literature in the University of the West Indies, Barbados, believes that Caribbean poetry, novels and plays are necessary in the curriculum of *all* schools in the region. He also agrees that our poetry can be taught very graphically by the use of visual and audio aids such as colour-slides, video and sound effects and music. He has also said that 'teaching plays without performing them, is like teaching chemistry without a laboratory.

page **4**. 'Lulu' from the LP album *Sparrow* (RCA LPB 9035).

page **4**. 'Man Dead' from the book of poems *Near Mourning Ground* by Victor Questel. He also wrote plays, reviewed theatre for the Trinidad newspapers, and was an acknowledged expert on the artistic works of Derek Walcott, the St Lucian playwright/poet. Unfortunately Questel died in 1982, before he could publish the book about Walcott he had been working on for several years.

page **5**. From a West African creator/destroyer god-figure, Ananse, who appears as a spider, and sometimes as a turtle. A god with a sense of humour, Ananse is known as a trickster. He occurs in many other cultures – the Dakota Indians of North America have a trickster god called Ikto-Mi

55

who is portrayed as a spider.

page **5**. Brer Rabbit, from *Tales from Uncle Remus* by American Joel Chandler Harris. Here is another trickster fellow. One of his famous tricks was to beg Brer Bear not to throw him in the briar patch (thorn bush), so in the end he was thrown in the patch, where he easily moves around without being stuck. That was in the story 'Brer Rabbit and Tar Baby'.

page **5**. *Anancy Cricket* is unpublished. It was told to Ken Corsbie in London, 1982.

page **5**. *Jumbie Picnic* is unpublished. Recorded during an All-Ah-We show, 1974.

page **8**. 'Cuss Cuss' from her book of poems *Jamaica Labrish* published by Sangsters, Jamaica, 1966.

page **8**. '*Dryfoot Bwoy*', ibid.

page **10**. 'Tanti at the Oval' from the book of poems *Tim Tim* published by Keensdee Production Ltd, Trinidad, 1976.

page **10**. Among the outstanding Caribbean soloists:
— Lloyd Reckord (Jamaica) who is a professional performer of Caribbean poetry, has done his one-man show in many of the islands, in England, Canada and America.
— Andrea Gollop (Barbados) who performs the works of a Bajan dialect poet, Jeanette Layne-Clarke.
— Michael Smith (Jamaica) who was one of the finest dialect poets until his unfortunate death in 1983.

page **12**. *Jouvert* (pronounced Joo-vay) from the french *Jour Ouvert* – opening day, or the start of the day. Jouvert morning is at four a.m. on Whit Monday, when many thousands of people gather in the streets of Port-of-Spain, and tramp through the streets to the beat of live steelbands. They stop at about eight o'clock in the morning, to go home and change into costumes for their all-day mas' band parade.

page **12**. *Jack* from a disco-45 disc of the same name by The Mighty Gabby Carter, 1982.

page **12**. Bus Man from the 45 r.p.m. record published by Farcia, 1983.

page **13**. *O Babylon* was published by Farrar, Straus and Giroux, New York, 1978.

page **14**. 'Bajan Litany' from 'Bruce St John at Kairi House' published by *Kairi* magazine, Trinidad, 1975. 'Bajan' is a familiar name for a Barbadian.

page **15**. *Boyhood Days* is just one of dozens of calypsoes which examine the Caribbean experience, and which were created by Dave Martin. He lived for 22 years in Canada, and somehow was able to continue to write these songs, which resulted in a new LP disc for almost each of those years.

page **15**. 'Revo' from the book of the same name, published 1976.

page **22**. 'Smile Orange' from *Old Story Time and Other Plays* published by the Longman Group Ltd, UK, 1981.

page **25**. *The Trinidad Carnival* was published by University of Texas Press, Austin and London. 1972. Hill's theory is that with carnival being the most theatrical event in the Caribbean, it is an endless source of inspiration and material for modern formal stage plays. See Chapter 7 on *Musical theatre*.

page **25**. List of plays published (but not necessarily in stock) from the Resident Tutor, Extra Mural Dept, UWI, St Augustine, Trinidad.

page **25**. *Ping Pong*, ibid.

page **26**. *Son of a Bitch* is unpublished.

page **26**. *Speak Brother Speak* is unpublished.

page **26**. *Calabash Alley* was published in 1973 by Freddie Kissoon, 38 Sapphire Drive, Diamond Vale, Diego Martin, Trinidad.

page **27**. *Time Longer dan Rope* was published by Frank McField, 1980.

page **27**. *Pantomime* was published with another play of Walcott's, *Remembrance*, by Farrar, Straus and Giroux, New York, 1980.

page **29**. *Nite Box* was published by Theatre

Information Exchange (TIE) in 1979. Alwin Bully's address is 75 Hillview Road, Roseau, Dominica.

page **29.** *Pelée* is unpublished.

page **29.** *The Harrowing of Benjy* is published by the Extra Mural Dept, UWI, Trinidad.

page **29.** *Ti-Jean and His Brothers* from *Dream on Monkey Mountain and Other Plays* was published by Jonathan Cape, UK, 1972.

page **29.** *Marie La Veau, In a Fine Castle* and *Charlatan* are all unpublished works.

page **30.** *Old Story Time* from *Old Story Time and Other Plays* was published by Longman Group Ltd, 1981.

page **30.** *Sleepy Valley* by Extra Mural Dept, UWI, Trinidad.

page **30.** *Teacher Teach 'er* was published by Theatre Information Exchange. 1980.

page **32.** Tuk-bands appear in slightly different versions in many Caribbean countries. They all have a similar style of rhythm and tunes, and their instruments are usually two drums and a cheap tin-flute. In Barbados, tuk-bands are usually seen around Christmas time, accompanied by a dancing rider-and-donkey costumed participant. In Guyana, where they are known as 'masquerade bands', the animal represented is a cow, and the accompanying stilt-dancer is dressed as a woman and called 'Mother Sally'. St Lucia's version ('Bamboo Melodians') includes the playing of a bamboo wind-instrument with a deep sound: meanwhile the dancer performs on two horizontal bamboo poles being manipulated by two other members of the group.

page **32.** Beryl McBurnie was one of the six Caribbean artists specially honoured at Carifesta '81 in Barbados. Among the others were Barbadian poet and actor Frank Collymore, and the Mighty Sparrow, who is considered by most people to be the greatest calypsonian in the world.

page **33.** Rex Nettleford is a professor at the UWI Jamaica, where he teaches Caribbean history.

page **33.** 'Modern' dance is a style which breaks away from the strict European ballet techniques, and frees the dancers to use their bodies more expressively. The pioneers of modern dance were the American women Isadora Duncan and Martha Graham. Todays' Caribbean dancers use this technique as part of their training and style.

page **35.** André Tanker wrote the music for Walcott's *Ti-Jean and His Brothers*, and also for the Trinidad film *Bim*.

page **36.** Cole Porter was an American songwriter of the 1930s and 1940s. He created hundreds of popular songs of the time with many of them being very popular in the Caribbean.

page **38.** *Pio Pio* from the Dominican children's chant used when they threaten one another for doing something they shouldn't have done:
Pio pio pio po.
I gun tell mih mudder dat tho.

page **38.** *The Joker of Seville* was published by Farrar, Straus and Giroux. The music was written by Canadian composer Galt McDermot who was famous for his music in the rock-musical *Hair*. An LP disc of many of the songs of *Joker of Seville* has been published by Semp Studios Ltd. Trinidad.

page **40.** *Banjo Man* is unpublished.

page **41.** Jab Molassi were the Devil's workers; they coated themselves with molasses and threatened to rub against anybody who did not give them some money. They wore pointed tails and carried three-pronged spears.

page **41.** Picong is the art of teasing or good natured insulting, usually by quick repartee, which the Trinidadians and many Caribbeans are able to do very easily. It originates from the french *piquant* or *pique* meaning stinging or taking offence.

page **43.** *Barbados Barbados* is about Rachel Pringle, a famous Bajan ex-slave woman who owned an hotel and nightclub in the 19th century. Corsbie directed it, using many styles including audience participation, extempo, sing-alongs, mime and character changes.

page **48**.   *Couvade* was published by the Longman Group Ltd, 1974. The couvade myth among some Carib Indian tribes is the belief that the father passes on certain attributes to the newly born child by suffering discomfiture or even danger during the birth. Among certain river dwelling tribes, the custom, it is said, is to tie the father-to-be to a tree trunk just below the high-water mark during the final stages of his wife's labour. If the birth is delayed, his own life becomes (symbolically, if not actually) forfeit to the rising water.

page **48**.   *Mother Poem* was published by Oxford University Press, UK, 1974. *In the Castle of My Skin* was published by Collier Books, UK, 1970. *The Dragon Can't Dance* was published by Longman Group Ltd, UK, 1979. *Dog* is unpublished.

page **49**.   Theatre Information Exchange: in 1984, the President is Alwin Bully; Vice-President, Geoff Cresswell; Secretary, Gem Madhoo of Theatre Company, Guyana.

page **50**.   *Kirnon's Kingdom* is unpublished. It was one of the plays first seen at the Playwrights' Conference in St Thomas, 1981. The story is of social change, political tensions, and family conflicts in an un-named Caribbean island.

page **52**.   *The Theatrical into Theatre* by African writer Kole Omotoso was published by New Beacon, London, 1982. It is the first book to attempt to deal with the growth and present status of drama and plays within the English-speaking Caribbean. It explains some of the African roots contained in our modern theatre.

Meanwhile, Errol Hill and Jamaican Wycliffe Bennett have been collaborating for years on the writing and publication of two books which will detail the history of the origins and development of the Jamaican theatre.